"The best how-to book of this nature that I've ever seen! Comprehensive, inclusive, thoughtful and all offered with a terrific sense of humor and constant empathy. A must-have for any writer seeking to set up an online creative writing class!"
FRED G. LEEBRON, DIRECTOR OF WRITING PROGRAMS IN CHARLOTTE, ROANOKE, GETTYSBURG, AND LATIN AMERICA, AND PUSHCART PRIZE AND O. HENRY AWARD RECIPIENT

"In this essential, timely work of nonfiction, Melanie Faith writes like a dear friend whispering in your ear. She is the online teacher's sage—a mentor who guides educators through the complicated, challenging, rewarding world of the virtual classroom. This unique book offers clear, detailed examples of how to succeed as an online instructor—how to give to our students, but also to ourselves. She presents online teaching as an art form, as she graciously shares her expertise and offers multiple opportunities for instructors to revisit and refine their craft. I will return to these glorious pages again and again."
GINA TROISI, AUTHOR OF *THE ANGLE OF FLICKERING LIGHT*

"The comprehensive, how-to, exercises-included guide is 'approachable, authentic, and comfortable' to use Faith's words to describe how to set up an online class that includes the shortest commute ever! A unique needs- and skills-based book that offers community, support, and passion in a down-to-earth, real-world way."
TERRI MCCORD, MFA. QUEENS UNIVERSITY OF CHARLOTTE, AUTHOR OF *THE BEAUTS*, TWO-TIME PUSHCART NOMINEE

About the Author

Melanie Faith likes to wear many professional hats, including as a poet, photographer, prose writer, professor, editor, and tutor. Imagination and possibility are her favorite sidekicks. She especially enjoys writing nonfiction craft books that assist fellow authors on their writing paths.

Learn more about her writing process, writing classes, and latest projects at: *www.melaniedfaith.com*

WRITING it REAL

Creating an Online Course for Fun and Profit

Melanie Faith, MFA

Writing it Real:
Creating an Online Course for Fun and Profit
Copyright © 2022 Melanie Faith

All rights reserved.
Print Edition
ISBN: 978-1-925965-78-0
Published by Vine Leaves Press 2022

Cover design by Jessica Bell
Interior design by Amie McCracken

A catalogue record for this
book is available from the
National Library of Australia

Other Books by this Author

Writing it Real: Crafting a Reference Book that Sells

In a Flash!: Writing & Publishing Dynamic Flash Prose

Poetry Power: Writing, Editing, &
Publishing Dynamic Poetry

Photography for Writers: A Writer's
Companion for Image-Making

Flash Writing Series Collection:
A Writer's Companion for Flash Fiction,
Poetry and Image-Making

Table of Contents

*For my fellow educators and my
students: past, present, and future*

"While we teach, we learn."
Seneca

About This Book: A Few Words of Purpose from Our Author

I've taught professionally in classrooms for over twenty years, and for several years I've also taught online as a freelance creative writing instructor, for a university as well as a creative writing school, and tutored both in-person and online at a college-prep school. There are some key differences between teaching online and teaching in person, which the COVID-19 pandemic and quarantine have made quite clear, as well as some old standby practices that are forever a part of pedagogy. Whether you're a first-time online teacher or a seasoned online instructor, I aim to spark fresh approaches and to inspire new ways of looking at the teaching art and the teaching of *this* art, writing. Welcome!

This book began as a four-week class that I created to teach online (surprise, surprise!) at one of the schools I work for; I've now taught the class several times with groups of students and as an independent study, with individual teachers in the US and from around the globe who were eager to break into online educating.

I road-tested the core of this book while teaching my pedagogy students online, and I am grateful for my students' feedback and enthusiasm in test-driving the exercises that appear in this book. Their responses and participation gave me a few light-bulb moments for additional online teaching tips I wanted to share and that also inspired me to expand several chapters.

I've included a series of four sets of exercises in the book that I encourage you to take for a spin, to spark your creativity and hone your class-forming skills as well. By the end of the four weeks when my students and I covered this material, students had a working syllabus as well as a focused, enticing class concept that they were then free to develop more and pitch to online schools. They also had the skills to choose to launch on their own website or platform. It's inspiring, the wide variety of awesome class concepts that arose from these exercises: from a course on writing children's picture books to classes combining regional cuisine and creative writing to creative writing classes for novelists and poets. The exercises are meant to be used again and again and to be elastic enough to encompass any sub-genres of creative writing; I myself used the exercises to create a class I've since taught online called Fundamentals of Graphic Novel Creation.

This book contains suggestions, tips, and resources to assist teachers of English and especially creative writing classes whose students are middle-to-high-school age, college age, grad-school age, and above. My aim includes using real-world advice while also offering many options and a variety of online pedagogical tidbits. I've done this because I know that each classroom, each student, each writing genre, each class, and certainly each instructor has their own approach and their own strengths as well as challenges to consider. Adapt this material to your own teaching life as you see fit.

While this book is divided into three parts, I've included thematic titles so that readers will locate topics at-a-glance that will spark their interest (particularly if in a hurry or lesson- or syllabi-planning). This book may be read chronologically or on a chapter-by-chapter basis as needed.

I encourage all readers to take the Self-Quest Survey about what fires you up about online teaching and to peruse the three interviews I conducted with professional online writing teachers whose authentic and varied experiences with online teaching offer much wisdom to consider.

In the end, I wrote this book to support, encourage, and share camaraderie with my fellow educators, and you are welcome to read this book in whichever way motivates you most.

You've got this. Happy teaching online!

Part One:

Tips and Topics in Online Teaching

Four Tips for Finding Your Perfect Class Theme or Genre

One of the easiest places to start building a class is to choose a theme or genre; it's the first step I take when I create my own courses and syllabi. Narrowing your course topic will make it clear to potential students the kinds of assignments they will write and what they can expect to read during your class.

Beginning with a theme or genre will also make it easier for you to plan your course syllabus. For instance, if I'm going to teach a short story writing class, then I quickly omit handouts or reading assignments that involve poetry or nonfiction in my planning. At the same time, I can also begin to craft short-story-related hand-outs, cull online video links and other short-story learning tools that will assist students' writing, start writing prompts and assignments related to short stories, and begin to narrow the specific elements of the genre we'll cover in my class.

Without picking a single theme or genre, it's quite easy to waste days (or weeks) sorting through endless lesson ideas and making a syllabus that is too long or too repetitive (boring your students to tears when what we need is to inspire their pens). Why make learning and writing harder for your students or yourself? Focusing on a single topic from the get-go is a time-saving and clarifying way to go.

With that in mind, consider these four tips:

Choose a genre you enjoy reading and writing.

Do you have a favorite poet? How about a favorite literary journal or short story or essay writer? The enthusiasm you feel for genres you most enjoy reading and writing will naturally show in a class you teach.

There are numerous genres in creative writing and literature; it would be impossible to list every genre class-idea possible, but here's a healthy, hearty list to get you thinking about the genre you'd most like to pick: flash fiction, novels, novellas, the longer short story (2,000 words or more), creative nonfiction essays, flash essays, micro-fiction, ekphrastic fiction or nonfiction (writing based on another art form, such as photos or paintings), free verse poetry, formal poetry, prose poetry, autofiction (a blend of nonfiction and fiction), and more. Then there are even more specific genre and commercial classifications that would make great classes, from YA comics or graphic novels, humor (such as jokes or essays), screenwriting, writing for theater and stage/plays, children's picture books, romance (of which there are endless possibilities from light romance to contemporary to romantic suspense to inspirational to YA romance to Regency to paranormal and speculative), thrilled, horror, dystopian fiction, historical fiction (again: endless types here; combine an era or place with historical fiction writing techniques, and le voila!), travel-based personal essays, writing science fiction and fantasy (again, endless class ideas within this genre to choose from), food writing, and myriad others that could become a marketable class concept.

See? The sky's the limit!

If you can't find the exact genre you want to teach, don't let that stop you—I didn't. Whenever I wanted to combine my love for writing with my love for photography but couldn't find a textbook that specifically approached photography from a writer's POV and focused on imagery in both genres, I sat down and created my own handouts that eventually became my book *Photography for Writers* and the assigned reading for an online class of the same name that I've enjoyed teaching for two or three years already.

What genre have you published in (most)?

While it's not required to teach in genres in which you've already published, it can be a helpful selling point for your class. Poets want to study with poets who know tips for submitting and publishing poetry; essay writers and short fiction writers also appreciate tips for writing, editing, and submitting from writers who have already submitted and published their own prose.

This way, you can also offer your fellow writers advice for what worked and, just as importantly, what didn't work for creating, editing, and marketing your writing.

Choose a genre you would like to explore more.

I plan my class syllabi a few months before I teach my courses. After teaching prose writing for a while, I'm raring to teach poetry for a while. Why? Variety. Why else? When I plan to teach a course, I actively read and also write in the same genre much more. A bonus for my upcoming class *and* for my writing and publishing careers!

When I discovered Creative Nonfiction (CNF) and flash memoir in grad school, I immediately wanted to study and share more examples of this genre, so I created two online courses ...

and began writing up a storm in both genres. I likely wouldn't have done so without the focus (and reading) that my class planning inspired.

Choose a genre that is themed or combined with another artistic genre.

Some of my favorite writing classes to create and to teach involve themes or combinations of genres. I've created and taught Food Writing, Humor Writing, Grief Writing, Poetry for Publication, and Photography for Writers courses for Women on Writing, a wonderful online writing school which offers year-round classes taught by writing and publishing professionals. They also offer writing contests, links, and craft articles to assist writers in meeting their writing goals. I have written in all of these genres, but I also have sustained interest in reading and sharing about these topics.

Consider creating a course that combines a genre with publishing skills or a genre with a visual or physical art. For instance, why not a writing class aimed at painters who need to describe their work for galleries and fellowship applications? Or a novel-writing class for runners and/or other athletes? Or a journaling class for cyclists or yoginis or softball players? One of my grad-school friends just created a writing class for law-enforcement officers. The combinations are exponential.

Determining Your Target Audience. Or Who Will Take Your Class, Anyway?

Consider age and/or educational groups. Will your class be pitched towards teens currently in high school or college? What about college graduates who want to take a non-credit class in their spare time? Or perhaps for graduate students or members of a writing group or club who may be a mixed audience of youth, adults, and seniors? A friend of mine teaches creative writing at a senior center. Another friend teaches twenty-somethings. Your students might be writers who have degrees in other subjects and have always wanted to write a novel or essays or poetry but might not have a basic foundation in creative writing and publishing. Consider crafting classes based on generational ties, if you know that your students are mostly or all from a single demographic, such as a class for Gen Zers, Baby Boomers, Millennials, or Gen Xers. All of these are target audience groups with a variety of outlooks and hopes for their writing projects. As you begin to choose a genre or theme and before choosing a class text or writing handouts, it's important to know the writing needs of your potential students. What authors will your students like to read/identify with most? What causes and/or groups do they belong to? What goals might students of a certain age or demographic have, and which genres are their favorites?

I currently teach for three different schools, which all have different target audiences. One school focuses exclusively on high-school writers preparing to go to college. Another school is for graduate writers studying for their Master of Arts in Creative Writing and completing a thesis book-writing project, with a wide age range, from mid-twenties through about early-eighties. Another school has many writers in their thirties, forties, and up.

When I choose supplementary materials (or write them) as well as class texts and other resources to share, I consider the unique needs and skill levels of my students in each class. My high school students often have not published, whereas many of my graduate students and Women on Writing students have been published or have at least submitted work already. I share information about publishing, editing, and writing with all three groups, but based on the needs and interests of my students, I hand-pick and hand-create the class materials slightly differently. Students who have already submitted in the past probably don't need instruction or examples on how to write a query letter to a literary magazine, but they might enjoy tips for improving their author bios, launching an author website, and writing a more-effective pitch to a literary agent.

Some writing markets and contests are aimed at one focused audience. For instance: many literary magazines seek work from emerging artists, which is an opportunity for writers of all ages and a perfect market to share with unpublished writers. Many literary magazines publish a specific age, gender, geographic or social and political demographic, such as magazines for high schoolers, for undergrads or graduate students, for BIPOC writers or women or LGBTQ+, for writers residing abroad and/or writers residing in specific geographic regions like Asia, the UK, Canada, or the American West or South.

In a group of writers with many backgrounds, skill-levels, and ages, I keep my eyes and ears peeled for specific resources I can share to meet the needs of as many of the writers as possible and which match with their particular writing styles and skills—this tip is helpful for once you have met your class.

Will your students have experiences in other artistic genres, too? Many of my creative writing students at all three schools have experiences in visual arts, whether photography, filmmaking, painting, music videos, Spoken Word, studio art, sculpture, or another artistic media. Knowing this, I often include a visual component in my class announcements and posts for most of my courses.

Will your students be interested in publishing at all? Many writing classes cover the writing and/or editing processes exclusively. Some students will produce art for their own satisfaction, to build their own skills, and for self-expression, so publishing doesn't always have to be a part of a creative writing class. You will draw other students to your class, though, *because* they hope to become published and to learn more about the submitting and publication processes. If you plan on addressing publishing, it's definitely something worth mentioning directly, either in your course description, syllabus, or both.

Will your students have submitted work and/or had their work published? When you write and pitch your course, consider that unpublished writers who have just begun to submit their writing and gather rejection slips will have different needs and goals than writers who have been submitting and/or publishing off and on for years. What did you most want to learn when you started submitting your work to editors? What advice would you give writers within your genre now, based on your experiences writing, editing, and submitting? I created Poetry for Publication to encourage and share what I know about poetry publishing (from indie literary magazines to chapbooks and small-press publication of poetry books) with poets just beginning their publishing journeys in the genre. A focused class topic, with the aim in the title, also helps to attract students who not only want to continue writing poetry but who want insider knowledge about how publishing verse is, in some ways, different from publishing prose.

Will your students be more interested in a more serious approach to the topic or a more fanciful tone? Sometimes, the genre influences the tone and the target audience. Most students in my Grief Writing class had either experienced deep personal losses or were healthcare professionals who counseled and assisted others in the grief process. Knowing this, I chose resources to match the serious and comforting tone that would encourage these writers in their healing process. On the other hand, students in my Humor Writing classes specifically hoped to encounter witty, quirky, slightly offbeat material that would inspire comedy from their pens, which I considered as I wrote, shared, and offered suggestions for their writing assignments.

Keep in mind that in accredited programs, students may be assigned your class by a registrar as part of their degree process, while for noncredit programs, students will often choose your class themselves from a course catalog, online listing, or ad and pay for classes individually. **Choosing descriptive, brief, and informative titles (and writing lively course descriptions—more on that later) to pull in your target audience can be especially important for increasing enrollment in noncredit or independently run classes.**

Narrow, and then narrow again! Consider specialized elements of the writing and/or editing process. Sometimes, instead of considering my target audience as a certain educational or age demographic when choosing materials and promoting, I consider a different angle: what skill (or few skills) will this class focus on sharing? I've created classes in Novel Outlining and Characterization and Imagery in Fiction. Rather than trying to cover the soup-to-nuts of writing a book as well as promotion, it can be a great idea to form a class around one or two specialized skills. Many online teachers focus on a general idea, such as writing personal essays, but far fewer create a class for submitting personal essays or specific tips for editing personal essays.

The Obligatory Pros and Cons List to Teaching Online. Or How Teaching Online can be the Bomb or a Dud

Here's the thing: teaching online is a different beast than standing right in front of your students. This is not to say that it's any better or worse than on-site teaching, but it is important to consider both the pluses and challenges that educators and students experience when moving class interactions onto a handheld screen.

Pros:

Convenience. Several of my classes are asynchronous, meaning that students and teachers can pop by any time of day and night to leave and answer messages and download or share content, so teachers and students can communicate frequently whenever a question or clarification opportunity arises. Even in my classes that are in real-time, students are welcome to email, text, or ask questions during our online session.

The commute is the best I've ever had. Two or three minutes tops! Who could ask for more? I've known teachers who were adjuncts (part-time teachers, often hired on a class-by-class or semester-by-semester basis) at two or three on-site colleges in different directions, and with a commute of at least an hour each way. One friend spent a few years teaching in the mornings at a liberal arts college and then driving over an hour in the other direction and teaching at a community college in the late afternoon or evening. He often ate fast food or a snack on the run between campuses and sometimes missed one or two meals entirely when his schedule included an afternoon, rather than an evening, class at the other school. Then, he also sometimes ended up with giant holes in his schedule, especially when he had an early-morning and a late-morning class on one campus. His house was just far enough away that to run home for twenty minutes in-between would be ridiculous but to stay on campus without an office meant he sat in the library for two hours before his next class. Ugh. Needless to say, scheduling (often determined by a registrar and campus facilities' needs) can be exhausting and frustrating. Great news! Online teaching gives you part of your day back—the navigating to and fro part. This is time you can use for your own writing, your lesson plans, or to take a break so that you're refreshed for your students.

Many online programs offer great instructor freedom to choose texts, a class topic, to develop a course, and hand-pick or write handouts of our own choosing. This kind of encouragement for unique and individualistic course content motivates and inspires instructors as well as student writers.

Community. Meeting and supporting fellow writers is one of the best aspects of online teaching. I regularly meet and make friends with creative writers from across the US and abroad who share many of my same writing and life goals, including keeping my own writing and publishing goals active and lively. Several students from my online classes have kept in touch with me over the years, long after our course together ended. Many students have taken more than one writing course with me as well. I greatly value sharing anecdotes and examples from our continued writing paths, whether in the classroom or in encouraging emails long after an initial course.

Support. Fellow online teachers are often quite generous with sharing tips about their online teaching experiences.

Support II. These writing students aren't just students—they are also often the generous audience for your future published works. It's really moved me that so many students I've taught over the years purchased and read my craft and poetry books or saw articles or poems that appeared in literary journals and reached out with positive feedback. Students have sometimes shared about my books on social media and offered to write blurbs for future work if I needed them. Online students who share a rapport with you often generously give their time, effort, and enthusiasm (and purchasing cash) to buy your writing and tell their friends about it—this is tremendously encouraging and humbling. Offering the same in kind, whether through supportive messages or buying power (I've often purchased former students' work), is an important gesture in maintaining community.

A highly flexible schedule. As a freelance teacher, I am free to go to lunch with a friend or to grade at two in the morning without waking at 7 a.m. to report to a classroom.

The pleasure of making another writer's path more informed and supported. Much of what I learned about writing and publishing during my first ten years as a freelancer and creative writer was through my own slow process of blunders and floundering around; it's very rewarding to offer fellow writers tips and then to receive email updates as they succeed on their own writing, teaching, and publishing paths.

Working within a creative discipline means that we are expected to continue making our own art. It always means a lot to me when students ask about my current writing projects. There is a respect and collegiality inherent when students and instructors practice the same art. I've had some very fruitful, candid, and encouraging discussions with students as we chatted honestly about the ups and downs and in-betweens of writing, editing, and publishing. It's cliché, but I learn almost as much from my students each semester as they learn from me.

Motivation for my own work. Nothing keeps me engaged in my own writing process like encouraging others in theirs. As I often tell my students and clients: "We're all writers in this writing journey together."

You can teach online from anywhere. Some summers, when I've traveled to visit my nieces, I've taught half or more of my class from my sister's Midwestern guest room; it's run exactly the same way as if I were sitting on the East Coast the entire time. Online teaching affords the teacher geographic changes of scenery mid-semester that are impossible with on-site teaching.

I get paid to talk about my passion for language and literature at all hours of the day and night. [Pinch me.] My sister and I had a conversation about employment this summer, and something she said startled me: "You are literally the only person I know who is actively pursuing a career in the exact two subjects you studied [creative writing and teaching]." Every day, I'm grateful that I get to work at jobs that allow me to share my knowledge in a fun, down-to-earth, direct way.

Teaching online is also wonderful if you, like me, are an introvert who enjoys communication but also needs some personal space and time alone to replenish.

Cons:

(Okay, you knew there had to be a few, LOL; unfortunately, these will get more space than the pros because they often need a little explaining.)

Teaching online is a highly competitive field. (Understatement alert!) **Prepare for perseverance.** Although I've been teaching in the field for a few years already, it took me almost two years to get my first online teaching gig. There's a line around the block and then some to get online teaching positions at both credit and non-credit schools, and the competition for freelance writers offering classes is just as competitive. Why? See the many perks above. I've had numerous friends who had on-site teaching experience apply and get rejected from teaching programs online. **Rather than let this discourage you, let it motivate you to demonstrate how *you* are the *best* candidate to meet the needs of your student writers. What sets you apart? How will your class give writers the marketable**

skills they need? Be prepared for no-thanks as you prepare your backup plans and your next course syllabi ideas until you get your yes that will follow.

Fatigue. As many classroom teachers have found during COVID and quarantine teaching online, it seems like it would be easy-breezy to sit in front of a computer and deliver lessons with students while wearing pajama pants if we want, but it can be exhausting to sit in one place for even an hour at a time. Body language and student-teacher interactions are different and sometimes hard to intuit online. Some online platforms allow students and teachers to screenshare texts and assignments while others don't, which is one of several challenges online teaching can bring. Taking little steps to make the home office or other space into a good background as well as make your desk and/or chair more conducive to long bouts of sitting can go a long way. It is often crucial *not* to schedule back-to-back classes in the same morning or afternoon as one might in on-site classes. The self-discipline to enforce breaks, even of five or ten minutes away from the computer, is another great way to combat sciatic, back and shoulder aches, and neck-muscle pain. Still, after a few hours of staring at a screen, even with interspersed breaks, even the most focused, in-shape teacher can find themselves a zonked-out thinker with the body of a pretzel from bending near screens all day.

Common conundrums of space sharing. Myriad considerations fall under this umbrella. Instructors with young children must consider the logistics and cost of either childcare or how, where, and when the children will be in the same room, for how long the children will remain quiet if that's a possibility, and work around their offspring's schedules and schoolwork. Who will use which area of the home and which computer or tablet, and how will that affect download and connection speeds? Do you have a roommate or spouse who also works from home? Where will they work, and how quiet will they be when you need to get work done? Also, will they distract you with lunches out or other fun possibilities that are not conducive to teaching in the middle of the day?

Maintaining motivation. With online teaching, you'll largely be on your own to keep in frequent contact with your students to encourage them and answer questions. It will be up to you to find a quiet space or to adjust when interruptions, however cute, wag or pounce their way into the frame while delivering a class. (Here's looking at you, Fido and Whiskers!) You'll also be on your own not to listen to three podcasts in a row, lose an hour on posts, and then binge-watch streaming cooking shows. I mean, I've *heard* from a reliable source that can really eat up a day and then you'll be grading at midnight again.

Welcome to my Sty! I Mean, Home Office: Another consideration for teaching online: the where. Look, students don't often see where teachers live or other details about our personal lives and vice versa unless we share them, much less the inside of our apartments or houses; it can be a bit odd for both teacher and student to cross those home-space boundaries. Prepare for a day or two of slight discomfort as your wobbly stack of unread books beside your worn-in sofa or your daybed where you throw your coats shows up in the frame for the entire class to see before you realize it's in the frame. Possibly just as weird for you: seeing where and how your students nest in their own home environments. Some good programs create pre-made backgrounds, including beach and garden scenes and cityscapes, but if you screenshare or use other online tools, many backgrounds revert to the interior of wherever you log in for class in real-time. A few chagrined students I know can verify this technological glitch.

Also, **consider possible sources of noise pollution when choosing your best location for online conferencing**. These can include noises such as nearby construction, a noisy stairwell, or adjoining wall, nearby bathrooms (toilets flushing don't make great music to teach by), kitchen mixers, vacuums, or other potentially noisy/distracting equipment. If you live along a train or bus route or if your house sits over an airplane route, the back patio might not be the best place to conduct your class or record a video. While some sudden noises are uncontrollable or very infrequent, it's a good idea to think through potential distractions; prepare to switch rooms if necessary. You might tune out noises that will frustrate or annoy your students.

Professor PJs: When we must physically teach from a school building or lecture hall, we often make more attempts to pull ourselves (and our thoughts) together and have a better work-life balance just by operating from a location that's not our dining room with the empty pizza box, bedroom, or home office. Remember those PJ pants mentioned above? Yeah. The thing about online teaching is that instructors still need to maintain professionalism. You might fairly ask, well, when we can walk to our home desks, fire up the computer, and begin to teach in five minutes, who cares what outfit I'm wearing? After all, our brain still knows the same stuff. True, and while it can be refreshing and fun to wear flip-flops or a favorite stained shirt because our students won't see it anyway, it can fray at professionalism and motivation after a while to have no signal that work is about to be done. At least once or twice a week, I make the extra attempt to wear one of my school outfits and shoes while teaching online, whether the class is in real-time or asynchronous. Even if I'm just answering ten student emails and posting an assignment to a discussion board, there's something about wearing the teacher outfit, applying my lipstick or lip gloss, and bothering to put on earrings that gets me into the right frame of mind to share knowledge. Wearing different clothing is a subtle, symbolic gesture that shows an additional layer of respect for yourself as a professional writer and towards your students. It can signal leadership and a subconscious shift from relaxation mode to work mode.

Online programs don't offer health insurance or benefits packages. You'll have to pay for health insurance on your own. This is often pricey.

Instability and the art of the constant hustle. Unlike tenured professors or full-time teachers in public schools, I have four part-time jobs ten months a year: two of them teaching online concurrently for different schools, one offline in a traditional boarding school in the evenings, and one as a freelance editor. Most of my teaching friends who adjunct online like me also have at least two, if not more, jobs concurrently. Sometimes, planned classes get canceled at the last minute for lack of enrollment at my university job, which lessens my already small salary. My freelance gigs tend to appear in my inbox in twos and threes, but then there aren't other freelance offers for six weeks or so at a time. **Freelance teaching is feast**

or famine—planning ahead for the ultra-lean times is a must, as is time and effort promoting your classes and your services as a freelance writer year-round via a website and social media.

Intermittent internet outages. Plan on it—the internet will have outages when least expected. Prepare a short message to send to students with instructions for resuming or rescheduling sessions or a backup plan for covering class materials on days when your internet or your students' Wi-Fi blinks or goes MIA for a few hours. It happens to all of us. I've had students in the pathways of blizzards, hurricanes, wildfires, and serving overseas in undisclosed military installations, as well as the more mundane cable and/or telephone pole outages that suddenly strike, often in the hours before a major assignment is due because life is "fun" that way.

Like most teaching jobs, I spend on average at least two or three hours a day, seven days a week, emailing students and posting for classes. This is part of the job for which there is no monetary compensation or time regained.

***

As you can see, there can be quite a few challenges to teaching online. Don't let these drawbacks dissuade you from teaching online. Consider them as meaningful obstacles that will prove how much you'd love to teach in this exciting medium and work around them.

It's important to consider the full picture of what to expect as an online instructor and to weigh the true qualities of the job against your own personality, life goals, finances, schedule, living situation, and expectations.

Qualities that make a great online instructor include but are not limited to:

Passionate about writing and genre. If you're not zippy, thoughtful, and interesting in delivery, why should your students be?

Flexible and organized. You'll be keeping track of not only your schedule but the schedules and assignments of all of your students, and the students will often have extenuating circumstances or ask for extensions.

Great sense of humor. People, ourselves included, are often inconsistent and juggling numerous impossible situations at once while trying to create art. It's HARD out there for creative peeps—**let's make our classrooms safe and joyous places to be makers.**

Patience. Students will sometimes ask a few times a day for clarification or additional support for their writing and/or editing processes. As instructors, we will often run low on energy, work over-tired, deal with family and personal emergencies, and struggle with low motivation yet persevere week after week.

Creativity and compassion for others and self. Online students have a variety of communication styles, and sometimes there is a slight adjustment while getting to know students' styles and needs, just like in a brick-and-mortar, in-person class. Without body language, it's sometimes difficult to know the tone of a student's questions in a text or email. Make the effort to bridge the communication gap. Reach out an additional time or two to students who express confusion or frustration about a class assignment or other elements of the course. Some classes will be lively and light-hearted while others will be near-silent and sullen, and almost every class will include a student who is unsure of why or if they even want to be in the course or should be and who could use additional encouragement. **For some writers, your class will be the difference between their continuing to write or their giving up hope in writing and/or publishing**—this is an awesome responsibility, but even more, it's a marvelous opportunity to make a difference in the lives of fellow writers and in the future of creative artistry. You are helping someone's writing dreams come true, step by step, in ways small and large.

Above all:
"A good teacher is like a candle—it consumes itself to light the way for others."
Mustafa Kemal Atatürk

What Fires You up about Teaching Online? A Self-Quest Survey

While there are no right or wrong answers to these questions, each question was written to inspire you to think about your own hopes, goals, and plans for teaching online in your virtual classroom.

Please: be as honest, direct, and daydreamy as you'd like. Answer them all, or choose a few favorites, in any order you'd like.

Feel free to get your favorite beverage, a cozy perch, a notebook or fresh screen, and answer the following questions in your own words for the next twenty minutes (if time limits are motivating for you) or as long as you'd like (if you really get rolling along and don't want to stop mid-thought).

1. What genres have you written in the past five years?

2. When you think about your own writing path, what style or genre of writing has most inspired you recently?

3. What genre or writing-related topic would you like to learn more about?

4. What excites you most about the opportunity to teach online?

5. What are the advantages, for you, of teaching online? What qualities will it bring to your life as a person, a writer, and a teacher?

6. What scares you just a little about teaching online? What are some positive steps you can take to counter these slight doubts?

7. How many students would be in your ideal online classroom? Do you tend to like larger groups or smaller groups? Why?

8. Would your ideal class include a text by an author, handouts you write, or a blend of both?

9. If you'll use a text by another author, go ahead and list two or three craft books about writing that have inspired your own writing process that your students may also find inspiring or do a little search for fun. I get nerdily into picking texts for all of my classes

and, twice, when I couldn't find the kind of text I wanted, I wrote my own.

10. Write a paragraph to introduce yourself to your ideal student who will take your class. Describe what brought you to teach this class online and something about your own writing journey so far. Feel free to share a dream for your own writing. Then, ask your delightful ideal student two or three questions you'd like to know about them. I wrote and offered this exercise to a client who was considering teaching online, and he found it very insightful to his writing process and picturing his targeted class audience.

Try these exercises:

Part One: Jot a list of three or four creative writing topics you'd like to share with other writers. These might include specific genres, like poetry, creative nonfiction, or short stories, or they might also include themed topics, like writing about health, writing about food, science writing, investigative journalistic writing, fan fiction, nature/environmental writing, writing about sports, writing about discount shopping, etc.

Part Two: Once you have your list of topics: free-write up to 300 words or make a list of ideas and writing experiences for each of your writing topics. When you finish, compare and contrast them to see which topics you have the most notes about but also give you the most excitement about sharing with others. You very well may use this list to determine your first (second and even third!) online class topic. Keep your list handy and add ideas for classes to it as you progress through this book.

The When, Where, and How: Tips for Choosing Length, Style/Platform, and Start Day for Your Class

Tips for Choosing Class Length:

Some schools will decide the length of your courses for you. The graduate program I teach for online sets their classes at ten weeks per semester to cover all course material and for students to complete a final project in most courses. Semester and/or course lengths often vary by school.

My freelance studies are often four, five, or six weeks long, depending on the genre and the needs of the students. My novel and essay courses often run five or six weeks, whereas my photography and poetry courses tend to run four or five, but pick the length that makes the most sense for the amount of material you want to cover in any genre.

If students want to work on a project during the class, consider longer classes rather than shorter ones to give the students time to complete parts of the project and/or to edit or workshop with other students to get feedback before turning in a final project.

Look at your personal schedule and determine how much time you have to invest, considering other life investments/responsibilities, travel, upcoming holidays, and the like.

Keep in mind that in many parts of the world, July-August and December are vacation times, which may affect students' availability, funding, or desire to take your course.

What style or platform of online class will you teach?

There are various formats for sharing content with students online, including but not limited to:

- email directly into individual or class list mailboxes (I often use this method for one-on-one independent study teaching)

- setting up a time to meet synchronously

- posting content (including weblinks or pre-recorded videos, etc.) on an asynchronous platform where students can log in at any time, day or night, to read and share posts/replies

Some online instructors like to use a variety of these platforms for the same class. For instance I often use my school emails for student questions and communications as well as for students to submit their assignments to me privately. I then use social-media groups or other online class platforms to publicly post additional class resources like quotes, literary markets, and articles to encourage the whole group at once.

Since I often have multiple classes as well as long visits to see my nieces in the summer, I prefer asynchronous classes—where work is posted or emailed without a set time schedule for class—but about a third of my online work is via platforms with very specific meeting times lately. Some online instructors I know prefer setting "office hours" and conferencing in real-time or video conferencing with students, which is certainly something that can work well for instructors, depending on your schedules or work preferences.

Whatever platform you use, remember that your students will be reading a screen and scrolling, so including visuals and breaking long paragraphs of texts into smaller units (whether that's paragraphs, numbered lists, lists using asterisks, or another method) is helpful to your writing students as they process your posts and handouts.

Choosing your class start day: One of the best parts of freelancing and teaching for an independent online writing school is that I get to choose a start day that works for my schedule.

I get Fridays and Saturdays off from my on-campus job tutoring high-school students, so I like to start many of my online classes on Fridays. I used to begin classes on Mondays, which I still sometimes do, but I began to realize that when I started classes on the weekends, students often had more time to jump in at our discussion boards to post and introduce themselves than when I started with Mondays.

Beginnings of weekends or weeks make the most sense with my schedule and work habits, but you can begin your class on a Tuesday, Wednesday, or any day you'd like.

Consider the other responsibilities and other part-time or full-time jobs you may have before choosing your online class day. If you work a job where weekends are your main money-makers, then starting on a Tuesday or Wednesday when you have more time makes sense. On the other hand, if you have a 9-5 Monday-Friday gig or homeschool your children during the week, then a Saturday start date for class might be best.

Also, as you consider a start day, think about how often you'll pop by your class discussion board or when you'll set aside time to reply to emails and/or make posts or videos for your students.

Are you a natural night owl, like I am? In this case, you might want to work on your content and emailing after the rest of the family goes to bed. If you're a morning person, then perhaps getting up at four in the morning before your daily commute or before the kids or grandkids wake to post and email when you're fresh and raring to go would be best.

The great part about teaching online is that most classes are asynchronous, so people can post and interact at their own pacing and according to their own schedule. The downside is that there will be emails and posts nonstop for the instructor. You will need at least an hour per day to answer texts or emails, likely more if you teach more than one class concurrently; this is time you don't get paid for, but which is necessary to your students' progress and good experience in your course. The more direct the teacher interaction, the more students generally enjoy and feel likely to participate well in a class. You do *not* want to be the teacher who opens their email box to twenty or thirty messages to answer at one time. Talk about daunting!

Deciding the time(s) when you'll log in to communicate directly with students will create a schedule that will help you to keep on track and reply in a timely way without being constantly on-edge or on-call.

Some instructors like to set their phones to get updates with pings all day long, but I prefer to check my students' message boards and messages twice a day—once in mid-morning or early afternoon and again after my evening tutoring job.

Fabulous, Unconventional You—Finding Your Perfect Fit: Accredited Program/School, Independent Program, or Freelancing

There are three basic venues for teaching creative writing online.

1. **Accredited programs**

2. **Independent (non-credit) programs**

3. **Freelance classes**

   Accredited programs—these are often colleges or universities where students must apply and enroll in order to earn a degree (AA, BA, MA or MFA, or PhD) in creative writing. These programs are assessed by an outside (usually government) organization and meet academic requirements and standards. Academic deans and registrars often decide which courses online instructors will teach based on an already-established curriculum for the program. Many schools with traditional on-campus programs also offer online courses now, which diversifies and expands the opportunities for online instructors. It's worth checking into your local colleges and junior colleges to see if they have any openings for online positions as well. I've had adjunct friends who taught at their home college's and junior college's on-campus programs and, within a semester or two, they applied and successfully transitioned into being an online adjunct. Many of these programs pay per class/semester, so you may very well have some semesters with high enrollments (and much more paperwork and grading) and some with lower enrollments. Accredited programs usually tell the instructors when the semester begins and ends; many independent writing schools use a variety of start dates that are up to the individual instructors' preferences. Accredited programs are often the most selective and often the toughest market to break into, but once you're in and prove that you are a reputable instructor who works well with students, accredited programs tend to invite instructors back to teach semester after semester, which can be both lucrative and fun. I've taught for a university for over five years now and love the variety of students' ages, backgrounds, and writing styles.

Independent (Non-Credit) Programs— these programs include students who will not earn a degree for their work, but they offer the majority of perks from an accredited program. For instance, students learn fundamentals of writing skills, tips for editing their work, work-shop or critique, marketing advice, and the like. An advantage of these programs is that students can cherry-pick the individual courses that match their writing interests and goals best (and take, for instance, all fiction-writing courses each semester). Whereas, in an accredited program, the types of courses students take must fulfill requirements for the terminal degree and often include several genres of courses, no matter the student's concentration. In my experience, teaching for a non-accredited program gives instructors more freedom to choose the class's theme and materials as well. The classes tend to be smaller, so you can get to know your students quite well and you'll likely have no grading since students don't earn academic credit towards a degree for the courses and you'll be able to invest plenty of time in giving your students detailed feedback on their drafts. These programs have an excellent following and marketing in place. These schools will spread the word via social media about your classes to a wide pool of writers who may be interested in your course, increasing your likely enroll-ment in a course. It's good to keep in mind that many programs deduct an enrollment fee from your earnings (often in the ballpark of 15-30% of the tuition fee from each student), although some independent writing schools vary on their payment policies—always inquire during or after the interview and before signing the contract to teach your first classes.

Freelance classes—Sometimes, going it on one's own can be the way to go. With this option, you are the captain of your own vessel, so to speak. Also, you get to keep all of your profits (before taxes of course—you'll have to deduct taxes on your own from your online salary when teaching online). It's never been easier to network online via social media and set up a website offering freelance classes. You get to decide all elements of the course, including all of your classroom materials, when your class will meet, and its duration, as well as what online platform you'll use for your class meetings. Many social media sites that you might already belong to have video-posting and synchronous meeting capabilities as well as private-group creation or privacy settings on content; some platforms also offer free and paying options with additional video or meeting-hosting tools. Of course, this freedom also means that you will have to spend more time hustling your classes to get the word out for more student sign-ups and hustle without the wide array of contacts independent and accredited programs have at your disposal. Get ready to be a go-getter.

I've taught at all three venues for online classes, usually concurrently; they each have their advantages and challenges, although I've enjoyed all three types of learning environments online.

When choosing what's best for *your* schedule and goals as an online instructor consider these insider tips:

Accredited programs frequently have a multi-part hiring process just like brick-and-mortar schools do, often including but not limited to: a phone and/or video-conferencing interview, outlining of your teaching philosophy, a series of essay questions from the school about your skills working with a diverse array of writing students, an updated CV/résumè, your college transcripts, a variety of recommendations from other teachers or writing professionals (which might include editors you've worked with), a list of your publications and genres, and a sample class lesson and/or syllabus. Start gathering these materials before approaching accredited schools, especially ordering your transcripts which can take days or weeks to obtain. Once initially hired, many accredited programs require a short training course about university teaching policies before offering new hires a first class. Granted, these are a lot of steps; on the other hand, well worth it for the relative stability of being offered courses consistently, the networking, the prestige, and the great group of students and fellow adjunct faculty you'll meet and build rapport with along the way.

That said: keep in mind that accredited programs' registrars offer courses based on a complex system and depending on student enrollment from semester to semester. Many courses in a program of study are not offered in back-to-back semesters. There may be some semesters when you are willing to teach but are not offered a course. This has happened to me a few times, and it's a bummer.

Accredited programs usually require that their professors/instructors have published within their field. Some programs require at least one full-length book, while others take literary journals or other publishing credits. University programs also require that the writers have an advanced degree—MA, MFA, or PhD—within their teaching field. I have an MFA; most of the instructors in my online MA program have PhDs. Most online accredited programs require an MA or MFA in creative writing or a related English field to teach undergrad writers studying for AAs or BAs.

Many independent programs, however, hire writers with a BA and publication credits. Have you edited or advised with literary journals, led or advised clubs, or hosted a writing circle? Published a lot? Make sure to mention these independent ventures that may set you apart from the other applicants. Independent programs will still want to see your sample class syllabus and synopsis, your CV/résumè, references, possibly your college transcripts, and your publication history, so assemble those items and keep them updated and on hand before applying. Non-credit writing programs will often require teachers to pitch their class ideas along with completed syllabi and reading lists to editors or a committee a few weeks or months *before* each semester starts or a few times a year. This is standard and a great opportunity for teaching a wide variety of writing courses that have always interested you. On the other hand, it's a lot of legwork and requires imagination and preparation. Set aside plenty of time for curriculum updates and course development; then again, on-site teachers are often quite used to these steps, so that will come as nothing new.

It pays to research just a bit. Before you apply to independent programs, pay attention to what they already offer in the current semester by stopping by their classroom course website online two or three times and reading the class descriptions and syllabi if they are posted. If their classroom offerings already list two or three classes in personal essay writing, then consider it unlikely that they will respond eagerly to your course on personal essay writing. Perhaps, however, they don't have a class in editing novel chapters—in which case, if that is in your skill set, it would be the better class to apply to teach.

Independent programs also like to see that their instructors have extensive experience within the field. If you don't have publishing credits in the genre you want to teach, I'd recommend that you begin submitting to literary journals online to get publication credits. Another way to show your dedication and skill within a field before proposing a class is to post two or three samples of your relevant writing on your website. Just be aware, should you choose this option, you won't be able to publish those pieces in literary magazines later, as they will likely be considered already published. Publishing credits from edited journals are considered better credits than online posts and portfolios.

I heartily recommend to my fellow writers who wish to teach online that they have some in-person teaching experience first. No worries if you've not taught, say, high-school English or freshman comp at a college. You can gain great teaching experience hosting a monthly writing group, volunteering at a local scouting or youth center by teaching a Saturday writing class or a one-day seminar on a writing topic, or offering a free two-week class in your community for senior citizens.

If you haven't taught for a while or aren't in a classroom setting on a regular basis, it can also be good to do a little volunteer teaching or tutoring to brush up on communication skills and the realities of teaching in the 2020s. Plus, it's plain fun to share one's skills in a variety of settings, and you can try the exercises and ideas you have for a class when you volunteer. Gather a group of five or six writing friends or friends-of-friends who live across the country, pick a textbook, some "homework," and writing exercises that you'll lead and complete together as a class once a week, say on Saturday afternoons online for three months, and le voila! Your very own workshop coordinating practice!

It's possible to teach concurrently for all three types of venues online (I do). I recommend that beginning online teachers start by choosing one of the three venues that best matches their goals, writing history, and skillset to approach first. Initially narrowing the type of venue you apply to will also keep the application process as streamlined and focused as possible. Once you snag one online gig, you can always apply to more as you go.

Ka-Ching! Ka-Ching! How Much Should I Charge for My Class?

Deciding how much to charge can be a conundrum. Several factors go into choosing a price if you're going to freelance. Here's a quick list of considerations, followed by some more in-depth analysis of these elements:

- How long/how many years have you taught creative writing? Have you taught a class like this before?

- How much have you published?

- How much does the school you teach at charge for similar classes? Some credit and noncredit schools will determine the fee with and/or for you.

- How long is your course? Generally, longer courses cost more than shorter ones.

- It can be a good idea to estimate how much time you'll spend each week critiquing assignments, writing, and sending messages and/or lessons. Some teachers determine price using this equation x the number of weeks their course will run.

- After your first online class or two, you might consider raising the price slightly as your experience level increases.

- Keep in mind, though, that too high a price/ price inflation can discourage or prohibit students who really want to learn but who might be short on funds. Researching what some online schools and freelancers charge and choosing a median price can be insightful and a great starting place.

- Ask a friend what they'd be willing to pay for a similar class after reading your syllabus. This is one of the best, most encouraging things I did before setting the price for my first class. Many times, we undervalue at first the skills we have to offer; it pays to check around before settling on a final price.

There are multiple factors that go into deciding how much to charge for your class. These are some guidelines that have worked for me but know that there are many ways one can choose a price for your course.

Also, keep in mind that if your accredited programs usually set student price and offer the instructor a flat fee per semester for teaching the class, you cannot choose your own listing price for the course. Some independent non-credit writing schools and freelance teachers who run their own courses often get to set their course price-point.

How much teaching experience do you have? This can certainly include offline teaching as well as tutoring experiences. If you've home-schooled your child or someone else's, volun-teered to teach literary seminars or workshops, or have done a lot of public speaking and/or readings of your writing, all of these experi-ences underscore your expertise in the field and can lead to charging a bit more for your class than if you have never taught a class offline or done any volunteer teaching or participating in literary events.

When I started to teach online, I had taught at in-person schools for ten years. While it's not necessary to wait that long, it can be helpful to have some teaching or volunteer teaching expe-riences because that adds to the expertise you can advertise in your bio as well as increases the price students are willing to pay to get your advice about their work and the publication process.

How much have you published? If you've published a lot or routinely, then you've no doubt picked up many types of experiences editing, composing, and getting rejections for your own work. You've learned about different types of editors as well as how to question editors who suggest you make changes to your work before publishing. You've also learned about how to put together a manuscript. You can market all of these skills [read: $kill$] and increase your value and what you can charge for your classes.

How much individual feedback will you offer students? If you are going to offer students individualized feedback on their drafts/assignments, as I do for my online classes, that takes extra time and energy than if students receive just a reading assignment and a post or two online. I've taken arts classes in photography online where very few students receive personalized replies to posts, and nobody receives an individual critique. Students very much value individual attention in their online courses. If you will offer feedback on more than one assignment, then you should take that into consideration when you set the price. If you offer both online posts *and* individual feedback, you should consider charging more than for courses which are not individualized.

I recommend that students research the price for several listed classes online, especially at the venue where you're interested in teaching. Look for how much the classes cost, how long the classes are (in weeks and days), and the resources (handouts, critiques of student work, etc.) that the instructor offers in return for the fee. Make sure to read the bios and publishing experiences for each instructor whose class you peruse. Then, set your class in the approximate value range but on the lower end of the classes that compare to yours. This way, you don't vastly underestimate your worth as a teacher but, on the other hand, you don't set the price so high that no one signs up for your course. After teaching two or three online classes, raise your price by a small amount, say $10-15 a class, until your classes are in the higher-value range.

I charge a little more for my five-week classes than my four-week ones, as students get an additional weekly critique of their work as well as more posted resources.

I've had teacher friends who offered their first class as a "Pay What You'd Like."

I've also known arts teachers who offered online courses where they gave a free week (sort of a try-before-you-buy approach) and then charged for the remaining two or three weeks of the course. Either of these ideas might be great for freelancers to give a try.

Ask honest friends, fellow writing pals, or acquaintances from your target-audience demographic what they've paid or would be willing to pay for an online class similar to what you want to teach.

Before I set the price for my first online class, I bounced the syllabus off a fellow writer friend from grad school. She loved the syllabus but circled the price and said, "No, you've under-valued your writing and teaching experience." Then, she named a price that was $30 more than I had listed. It can be very helpful and encouraging to get opinions about whether you might be charging too little or too much.

In the end, the price you set is your choice, but several or all of these tips will help you to tabulate pricing that would pay for the time, energy, writing experience, and enthusiasm you will invest into your course planning, your class, and your students.

To Market You Go: Practical Ways to Market Your Writing Classes and Increase Enrollment and Revenue

Your author website or blog. Your web presence is your prospective students' introduction to you. Update it often. For all three types of teaching, keep your blog and/or website up to date. Editors, Deans, and others who interview and hire for online teaching jobs often peruse these sites to see what you're up to with writing and publishing. For freelance teaching, count on your students looking online to see what you write and publish and if you are active in your art before they sign up for the class. Many students who find abandoned or infrequently updated blogs and websites will move on to the next class or instructor if it's a freelance or independent program class. I invest in a website and keep a blog that I update two to three times a month with upcoming classes, publication news, links to newly published work, and other writing and teaching-related updates. I include the link to my website with my author bio in my classes' advertisements.

Social media networking. If you freelance teach, consider amping up your networking process, as you will be the sole person in charge of making sure students can find out about your class. Perhaps post three or four tips that you'll use in your class on social media with a link to your class and details about it on your website. There are hashtags, such as #writingadvice, #writingpractice, #writingcoach, #writerscommunity, and #amwriting, that are useful when marketing writing-related materials to increase the visibility of your writing-class posts. Consider posting several times a week with topics related to your class theme, including the link to your upcoming class. Consider offering a discount for students who recruit their friends to join in or a slight discount on their next class with you. Join or start writing groups online (see below) and share the word there.

Form a social-media group that's writing-related. Social media groups make it easy to create a writing-related group and choose whether it's public or private. Then invite your writing pals and friends-of-friends to join as you share quotes, links to writing projects, favorite books, and more. In my private Writers' Conference group—made up of over

250 colleagues, writing friends, grad-school pals, and assorted writing students— I post many literary markets looking for submissions, quotes, and links to my upcoming classes. Giving this free content five or six times a week often pays back in dividends later when writers either take a class of mine or generously recommend my courses to a friend, ask me to freelance edit, or share writing opportunities with the group.

Treasure your pals. Ask willing friends to help spread the word with posts on their social media, as they likely have many contacts that you don't who might be in the market for what you offer. Make sure to offer the friends promotion in kind or lunch or a special treat, such as a favorite book or movie or gift certificate, in return for their support and networking.

Your author bio during publications. When journals and magazines accept your work for publication, it's customary for the editors to run a brief bio, which often includes a link to your website or blog. What better way to connect with like-minded writers within your genre than for them to notice on your bio that you teach.

Consider buying an ad via an online writing magazine or the back of a print or online literary journal. I've done this a few times for two of my books; through one ad, I made a talented new friend who not only bought two of my books, which was super kind, but also generously emailed me an opportunity that led to an additional publication. Consider the dividends of an ad being both potential increased enrollment *and* the networking possibilities inherent in advertising your class. You never know who your ad will reach and what new friends you'll make.

Start a newsletter and/or an email database. Many writers and teachers develop an email database over time with interested former students, writing colleagues, and writers met at conferences, workshops, or classes. I have a list of about 125 writers that I send short email updates or a newsletter (depending on how much time I have) that includes links to my upcoming classes, publications, a writing prompt, and more. I send these short updates around four times a year. Since they are personal email addresses, I tend to share less with this list than my social media to keep from bombarding their inboxes too much. Also, former students wish to be taken off of the list now and again; don't take it personally—we all get way more emails than we need. On the other hand, I usually get between one to three more sign-ups for classes just by sending an email update—well worth the time. Many students like hearing from the instructor personally, and I often encourage my former students to feel free to spread the word about my classes if they'd like. Several times a year some students "recruit" their pals or even family members for my classes, and nothing makes me happier.

Try these exercises:

Part One: Free-write up to 300 words or make a list or chart comparing and contrasting the various styles/platforms for online classes as well as the kind of start days/dates that would best work for your schedule. Keep in mind that some online classes use numerous styles (including videos and typed, posted content) within the same class. List all methods of sharing content that you feel confident using and/or could learn.

Part Two: After you've read "To Market You Go ... " pick at least three of the seven suggestions for marketing your class that would best work with your contact list, your personality, and your teaching style. Briefly explain why those methods would work best for your class. Feel free to add any marketing ideas/venues that occur to you during the course, such as advertising in local cafes or mentioning your upcoming online classes at Spoken Word/open mic nights. The sky's the limit!

Determining Your Objectives and Goals for Your Online Class

This is one of the most exciting parts of a class to put together. While you've probably never felt enthused by the almost-clinical term "objectives," now's the time to rethink all that the term can mean for your class.

Objectives can:

• promise your students what they can look forward to learning.

• clarify what you want to share most.

• narrow or omit extraneous or off-topic material.

• provide a framework for how you will pace your class from week-to-week.

Pretty heady stuff, no? I think it's very helpful to see first-hand examples of objectives, so I've included a list of objectives I wrote about a class I taught with the same theme as this book.

4 learning objectives for Creating an Online Creative-Writing Class for Fun and Profit:

1. Students should begin a list of possible topics for both a course they will explore more and start to develop during this class and continue to add course ideas that they might pursue in the future.

2. Students will learn many practical tips for how, where, who, and what to market in order to make money from their online teaching.

3. Students should be encouraged to pursue online teaching, matching their skills with a good venue (whether accredited schools, non-accredited schools, freelance teaching on their own, or a blend).

4. By the end of the course, students should have a draft of a class syllabus they can continue to work on after the class to pitch to editors or schools or launch their own free-lance class after the class.

Of course, there are many, many other goals I could have listed, but these main four helped me to stay focused and inspired many of the weekly writing assignments I wrote and shared.

An exercise I recommend to my fellow teachers before picking their class objectives: sit down with a blank document or a pad and a pen, and once you've chosen a class theme from your list, write a quick list (in fifteen minutes or less) of ideas for your class.

For the time being, don't worry about the order of your ideas or if the thought will match the theme perfectly. Just jot thoughts related to your theme or genre and how you might teach it as it occurs to you, drifting up like bubbles in the wind, letting them arise in time to write them down and let them go. You can pick favorites later.

After you have a working list from your fifteen-minute free-write, likely of between five and ten items, ask yourself:

• What, specifically, do I want students to learn about this topic?

• What tangible assignment or project will help students to consolidate the skills we're discussing? In other words: how can they take the next step in their writing?

These questions will help you zero in on the most important takeaways your students will learn and to omit assignments and/or tips that might be interesting but that don't help students to accomplish their ultimate goal (in this case: the final, marketable sample syllabus that they can work on and pitch after our class).

Notice that my objectives involve specific skills and action steps students can take during the class to build confidence (objective three) and to strengthen syllabus-writing and class-launching skills (objectives one, two, and four).

Be as specific as possible about what you hope students will learn from you *and* the "how"/the methods they'll take (in assignment writing, sharing posts, watching videos and responding, and fill-in-the-blank methods here). Once you write your objectives, you can use them to inspire your syllabus-writing.

The great news: there are myriad forms of sharing information in online classes so that students can easily find success in meeting your objectives.

11 Diverse Ways to Help Students Meet Your Course Objectives:

Offer individualized feedback on student drafts and/or assignments. I like to offer weekly feedback to students on their assignments to underscore areas they are doing well and give them constructive yet supportive suggestions that will improve their knowledge. I can also gently course-correct any misconceptions or errors. Some instructors offer feedback only once during the course or more frequently, such as every other day. From the other side of the desk, I've been in online classes that don't offer any individualized feedback; to be honest, I didn't like that approach as a student because even a morsel of instructor attention could have vastly improved my art. Determine what feedback schedule would work best for your class topic as well as your schedule.

Reach out to individual students via email or text or group-answer students' emails/texts within twenty-four hours whenever possible. This takes more personal time, but I like the caring, individualistic touch. Also, I invite my students to email me questions that they might not feel comfortable sharing in public on a message forum. Students bond with an instructor who goes the extra mile.

Write your own handouts with encouraging tips and advice. I clearly enjoy this method. You already know a ton about your subject matter, and handouts can be a clear, easily shareable, helpful way to share tips online. When I created my *Photography for Writers* class, writing the handouts so inspired me, alongside the great class discussions, that I ended up expanding the handouts into a full-length craft book.

Record short audio or video messages. Some instructors love to record their lessons verbally. Many cell phones make recording video clips quite easy to create and share. Honestly, this is my least favorite method of sharing content, as my cell phone is ancient and

I prefer typing, but several of my fellow instructors prefer recording extemporaneous videos to crafting written handouts and/or sending emails. To each their own! Do you, boo!

Provide examples from your own writing. I do this often in my online classes. In fact, I just shared four of my own course objectives (see above) as well as later sharing one syllabus with instructional margin notes that you can use as a template, if you want, for your own course-creation syllabus writing. Seeing how someone else approaches a writing exercise or how they brainstorm can often awaken fresh ideas for (stuck) students.

Share instructive/related videos or audio/ podcast links from other writers. I love sharing literary video clips from social media in my online classes. Video content doesn't have to be handmade by you to be authoritative, lively, and inspiring to the class. Also, you can save a *ton* of personal time (especially if making videos isn't your favorite thing) by sharing content already online by professional writers and teachers. Just make sure to give credit and the links so that students know the source of the content.

Share thematically related articles about the writing genre or weekly theme from online blogs, newsletters, and the like. Thanks to the internet, there are thousands of possible articles available for free or nearly free that will inspire your students. One of my favorite databases for reputable, informative creative writing how-to articles is *Writer's Digest*.

Include related imagery. I'm a very visual learner; I like to include photos, literary cartoons, or other imagery that inspires in my handouts and online posts. Many times, I use my own photos. Sometimes, I include the free clips from my word-processing program, while other times I use photos that are free-share licensed for use by anyone. My favorite photo source for free-share photos is the database *Unsplash*. They have a search engine that includes endless themes and many high-quality, intriguing photos on almost any topic you can think of; as a courtesy to fellow creators, include the name of the artist and mention the web link for any photos used.

Encourage students to post on message boards or platforms. All of my Women on Writing classes have a message board that is open only to students. I post there each day (often twice) and encourage my students to share their drafts-in-progress, writing shop talk, and quotes to form a community as a class. These groups are often one of the students' favorite ways to build camaraderie as a group and feel more like an interactive class. Students also ask insightful, clarifying questions and post resources for each other, such as writing markets or articles related to reading assignments that every writer (including me!) benefits from—win-win. While connecting/posting in my classes, several students have formed friendships and found beta readers and/or writing swap buddies to share their drafts after class—another great outcome from online sharing as a collective group.

Choose multiple methods. I was a student in a photography class online one summer where the instructor posted lessons on a webpage that only students could log onto. She also, once a week, did an online conference for about a half-hour where she answered student questions about the week's lesson and gave additional tips. Every other week she also included a five minute pre-recorded video walking us photography students through her creation and editing processes for two of her photo compositions, explaining why one photo worked and the other taught her lessons to apply to future photos she'd take. Such comparisons were highly informative.

Take an online class (or three) yourself. Although I'm an active online instructor, I've also taken several online photography and writing classes as a student, including an inspiring course last month on autofiction. Taking part in another instructor's online course will often inspire new teaching methods and technological tips for sharing information as well as offer insight into what your own students experience from your instruction. There's nothing like participating in a workshop to get my words flowing and to make me appreciate my students' bravery in sharing their fresh drafts! Plus, it's fun. And let's be real: there's nothing like a weekly assignment deadline for motivation—whichever side of the desk you sit on—to get those words in formation. In addition, any knowledge you learn will benefit your own students in future classes. Win-win.

Composing an Instructor Profile or Bio with Personality Plus

As teachers, we are trained to focus on others, with good reason. When teaching online, however, it's especially vital that your bio reflects your personality and your passion for your subject matter. You won't be standing in front of your students in a physical classroom for them to get a feel for your body language and, in the case of asynchronous courses, they might not even hear your actual speaking voice, so providing a dynamic, assured written presence for your students to get to know you is crucial to online teaching.

Your written bio, therefore, should reflect your three-dimensional teacher qualities as well as your individual personality that fellow writers will connect with during your time together. In my teaching experience and from anonymous student-survey feedback, most writers care almost as much about finding a potential writing mentor and writing teacher they click with as they do about course content and getting individualized feedback—your personal presence online is *that* important to students. Let's make it snazzy and inviting.

What details could you include in a memorable instructor bio?

Types of genres you've written and/or the names of publications where you've published work in the past few months or years.

How long you've taught. It's okay if this is your first online course—list offline courses and/or years that you've taught or volunteered, or even share with refreshing candor that you're excited to bridge into online teaching with this course.

Note your in-progress writing project(s). (I often do this). Students are curious to know what you spend your non-teaching hours writing. Sharing a brief few sentences or a paragraph about your current projects underscores that you, too, are a working writer that constantly practices their craft. It also sometimes happens that some of your students today will buy a book or two from you tomorrow.

A detail or two about **why you love creative writing**, especially the genre you plan on teaching.

Favorite authors and/or books within the genre you're teaching.

Who or what inspired you to teach creative writing and/or become a writer? That teacher or librarian in fifth grade who introduced you to the Beverly Cleary books that made you aspire to be a writer? Totally valid to give a shout-out.

Where you're from or currently residing and what is unique about that place/city/town/state. Do you reside in the Potato Chip Capital of the Midwest but grew up in the Grand Canyon State? It's these kinds of geographic taglines that set you apart and give students glimpses into your background as well as details they might not otherwise have guessed about you. Don't we all prefer the quirky teacher with personality to the blank-slate, who-is-this-person robotic instructor?

Name your degrees (especially your latest one that applies most to your class—I usually list my MFA) and/or where you went to school (I often note that I am a graduate of Queens University of Charlotte's MFA program).

Some fun and/or funky details that demonstrate you are a unique person, which might include: other hobbies (I frequently mention my penchant for photography and the fact that I collect costume-jewelry pins), **favorite vacation spot** (are you a beach person, a mountain person, or a city person?), **sports** (are you a cyclist, a yogi, or boxer in your free time?), **a detail or two about your**

family (I often mention "my darling nieces who live too-far away in Missouri;" you might mention your **fur babies, your partner or spouse or significant other, your children, your best friend for the past sixteen years**), or **even your funniest rejection anecdote** (I sometimes have a line in my bio about receiving "enough reject slips to wallpaper a small condo").

A few guidelines for writing your instructor bio:

Between 100 and 250 words is standard length. Shorter is often more-appreciated than longer. Keep it scannable but warm and welcoming.

Write and keep two different drafts of your bio at-the-ready—one for social media posts or literary journals that is smaller and a longer one for your website. I frequently have at least two drafts of my bio.

Update your instructor bio once or twice a year to keep things fresh, especially if/when you collect [more] publication credits and teach new classes or have significant life events that define who you are as a person (say: you got married or divorced, had or adopted a child or a first grandbaby, moved halfway across the country or to a new country, decided to take up quilting or to sell your jewelry online, or started to volunteer for a cause you feel passionate about in your local community).

Keep a balance between professional and personal details in your bio. All professional, and you risk looking stuffy. Too chummy, and you risk looking unprofessional. My own rule of thumb is 2/3 professional details (related directly to writing, publishing, and/or teaching) and 1/3 quirky or fun.

Share, but also use a little discretion. Your bio is not the place to note that you can't believe someone gave you this job or that on a dare you took part in a wet t-shirt contest in college or that you've had a miserable, bad-luck filled year or that you abhor your ex for recent shenanigans they pulled, even if/when these things are true. This isn't a tell-all or a rant. Bios can be a little quirky, but keep 'em classy, too.

Tips for Your Instructor Photo

It's also important that you have an up-to-date instructor photo that welcomes students to your class (and for your website and promotional materials).

Digital cameras and online software make it virtually foolproof to craft an instructor-bio shot that resembles you at your best. As an introvert and writer, I much prefer being *behind* the camera to in front of it, yet we don't need special makeup or clothing (or plastic surgery) to make a thoughtful author photo.

Put on your favorite outfit (you know: the one that's your go-to when you get invitations or that you wear for a night out with friends or a significant other), select a lovely outdoors location (a park, big backyard, or gardens often work well) or a plain-colored indoors backdrop/wall, and look for a diffuse light-source to avoid harsh shadows (everyone looks great with soft, natural windowlight and near "golden hour" just before dusk), and then snap away! Black-and-white can be artsy and fun for author photos, too.

Closer-up shots (torso-up or shoulders-up) tend to work better than whole-body shots, but use whichever you prefer. Front (camera-facing) shots are most inviting to viewers. Even a close-up selfie taken on a phone if you're smiling warmly and naturally can be a great greeting to your students.

Photography is my other passion, and I own a tripod, software, and both digital and film cameras, so I take most of my own instructor photos. One notable exception: last year's author photo was taken at the beach by my dad. Ta-da! I'm wearing no makeup, but I love my French-ish striped shirt, my holiday sunhat, and the sliding doors of the beach rental, and I look interested in life, so it won.

I took one of my latest author photos. The gray in my shirt matches the weathered gray, textural surface of the shed I'm standing near. When I spotted the visual interest of the wood's wear and the color mesh between the surface and my shirt, I knew it would make a great backdrop. I took the photo a few times in the late-afternoon light, using one of my small digital cameras. Technically, it's a selfie, folks. I chose the photo that is eye-level and where my smile is most relaxed and welcoming. Clearly, backdrops don't have to be fancy to work well, and you don't have to spend a lot of money, planning, or time to take a good one or to update an older shot.

The important thing about author shots is that you look approachable, authentic, and comfortable with who you are. Although it sounds counterintuitive: avoid bright, direct sunlight; it creates sharp shadows and dodgy burns and squinty winces on people's faces—none of which you want.

No worries, though, if the first shots aren't your favorites. I often take twenty or thirty shots before getting one I like well enough; many professional photogs take numerous as well to get one great shot—it's very common. Take as many as you want/need—no one else will know.

Keep it reasonably current—don't use a photo from five or more years ago. I update my profile photo and bio on average every nine-to-twelve months, often sooner. These photos are handy to have ready-to-go for a contributor's photo to literary publications as well.

If photography's not your thing, no problem—there's likely a friend, colleague, or family member who would be more than willing to help you craft a great instructor photo. For my university instructor profile, I use a great photo of me in a cheerful pink shirt at my desk that my elder niece took.

Also, consider the barter system: a dear writing friend and fellow online teacher swapped her copy-editing skills with an experienced local photographer and, in that way, got free professional photos for her online class and website.

She, in turn, gave great editing value for the photographer's updated promotional materials. Win-win!

Live on a shoestring budget? I hear ya! Good news: hiring a professional photographer can also be done on-the-cheap with a new photographer just breaking into the business—ask around. Many talented photographers just launching their businesses (especially high-school or college-age students with artistic vision, enthusiasm, and tech skills galore) will work for a smaller fee than studios (sometimes even for a donation) and/or for photos for their portfolio, making it a worthwhile experience for both writer/teacher and photographer.

Or if someone you know is considering launching their own small business but has yet to take clients, offer to be their first commission. You'll be doing a good deed in building up a fellow artist and you won't have to deal with the photo equipment yourself or feel awkward taking numerous selfies. Treat this photographer well by recommending them to possible clients and/or friends later and by giving them credit on your website and promotional materials and/or linking to them on social media.

Sample Syllabus

Sometimes, it's super helpful to have a direct example of how another teacher put together an online class syllabus to get ideas or a template to apply to one's own class.

Here's a syllabus I wrote for an online writing course, accompanied by explication of the techniques and tips I used:

In a Flash: Writing & Publishing Dynamic Flash Prose Workshop with Melanie Faith

Note: The title of my course includes the genre (flash prose) as well as two of the major areas we covered in the course: writing our own flash fiction and/or nonfiction as well as tips and advice specific to submitting and publishing flash. The word "Dynamic" suggests writing improvement and marketability, two great selling points for a writing class.

Start Date: Friday, April 16, 2021

It's helpful to students to know upfront when the class will begin, so that they can plan ahead and/or check their calendar for obligations they might already have.

Duration: 5 weeks

Since courses can vary in length, I like to state the length near the front of my syllabus.

Location: Private group (link sent on the first day of class) and email communication via the address each student provides when registering for the class

Students need to know where and how you will communicate with them to conduct class as well as if you plan to message students directly.

If you plan to share recorded videos or schedule a specific time and/or day for your online class to conference in real time, this would be a great place to mention these details.

Feedback: weekly instructor feedback of exercises via email

Spell out how often you will provide direct feedback on student work as well as how students will receive that feedback, whether posted at a group site, privately sent via email or text, or another method.

Course description: Flash is a dynamic, fun genre that more and more editors seek. Both flash fiction and flash nonfiction share many of the same qualities, from characterization and setting to conflict and dialogue. In this five-week workshop, we'll explore this eclectic art form and everything you'll need to have a lively flash-writing practice, from where to get ideas and drafting to editing and submitting your work. We'll discuss practical tips and techniques along with inspiring exercises from our text, *In a Flash!*, by Melanie Faith. Students will submit drafts weekly for constructive and supportive instructor feedback. There will be a private group for students to discuss the literary life and for sharing of literary resources, such as markets and quotations about the writing process. Topics covered will include: Begin Where You are; To 'I' or Not to 'I?;' Quotation Power!; "Flash," You Say? Four Tips for Compressed Dialogue; Villains and Vamps: Crafting Realistic Antagonists; Writing Private People; The Big Cs; Snapback: Incorporating Details of Era and Setting; I See You: The Value of (Re)Connection; Spark, Spark, Light! The Inciting Incident & You; Mixed-Emotion Station; Descriptive Ruts; Attributes: Adventures in

Style and Syntax; Idiomatic Time Travel and All that Jazz; The Advocate: Personality Types and Your Protagonist; The Whiplash Compliment; FOMO: Fear of Missing out & Your Characters; Tight-Roping: Balancing Self-Revelations with Self-Protection; Joy Bombs: How to Write Happy without Turning Your Reader against You; Playing Genre Ping-Pong; The Strategically-Shattered Plate; and much more.

Your description is the place to sell both what students can expect to learn as they write and how that information will strengthen their writing, especially if they choose to seek publication. Sometimes, I open my descriptions with a quote from a writer within the genre of the course. In this description, I mention the "fun" (self–fulfillment) as well as the marketability (by noting how editors seek this compact genre). Also, I list some thematic topics we'll cover each week as well as the name of the text, in this case a book that I wrote. I usually write the thematic part of the description once I've determined the specific topics I'll cover each week. I picked a handful of topics, since all of them will be listed below in my week–by–week description and to keep this description shorter.

I often run my course descriptions through two or three drafts, stopping to ask myself: Does this sound like a course I'd want to take? Which parts appeal most? Which parts sound dull? I revamp the dull spots as I edit the description.

Weeks at a glance:

I often highlight due dates in red font, to make them stand out for students who are scanning for this information to mark on their digital or print calendars.

Friday, April 16, 2021
(class begins)

Friday, April 23 and 30, and May 7, 14, and 21, 2021 (student drafts due for instructor comments)

Week one: The Three F's: Fast, Flexible, Fun; Begin Where You are, To 'I' or Not to 'I?;' Quotation Power!; "Flash," You Say? Four Tips for Compressed Dialogue; Villains and Vamps: Crafting Realistic Antagonists; Impressionistic Leapfrog: A Prompt in Naming; Brava, Pecunious, Grapple, Skulk: Jazz up Your Writing; Color Magic: The Power of Hue Imagery; Shrug Your Shoulders. Toss Your Hair; Stuck in Muck; and Spontaneous Song

To create a title, I list the week number alongside the themes covered.

In a Flash! **Text Reading:** Introduction "Why Write Flash? From Flashbulb to Snapshot on the Page," and all of section one: pages 9-53.

I like to include chapter or section titles (if the text has them) as well as page numbers. Including chapter or section titles is especially important since some of your students will buy the digital version of the text, which often either doesn't have page numbers or which might be numbered differently than the print edition.

Assignment: Write a flash (750 words or fewer) based on a prompt of your choice from the end of any chapter.

Be as specific as possible about your expectations for homework. Note if you want homework turned in on a certain day and/or in a specific format or program/app. If you have a certain maximum length in mind, list it. Students in this class were welcome to pick a prompt of their choice from the weekly reading prompts listed in the text; if you have a specific prompt or details for the assignment in mind, write it in this part of the syllabus.

Week two: Spotlight on Nonfiction—The Pivotal Moment; That's a Wrap!: Closure in Creative Nonfiction Flashes; Introvert Meets

Extroverted Art; Birthday Twin; Caught or Not? Reconstructing the Pieces; Amalgamation Station: Writing Private People; The Big Cs; Snapback: Incorporating Details of Era and Setting; I See You: The Value of (Re)Connection; Tender Underbelly; On Commemoration; It's [Not] Over; Scent: The Little Sense that Could; Wobbly Tree; Snap Judgments & Reversals; Emerald and Ruby Gelatin Cups: The Wants and Gimmes, and More.

In a Flash! **Text Reading:** Choose ten or more short chapters from Section II, "Get Real, Crafting Flash Nonfiction," pages 53-143.

Assignment: Write a flash based on a prompt of your choice from the end of any chapter.

Week three: Spotlight on Fiction I—Spark, Spark, Light! The Inciting Incident & You; Mixed-Emotion Station; Bye-bye-bye; Cleaning-Sponge Cakes and Other Misinterpretations; Shine Light on Broken Glass: Descriptive Ruts; Attributes: Adventures in Style and Syntax; Idiomatic Time Travel and All that Jazz; Keystone: The One that Got Away; Correspondences; Your Protagonist's Treasure; The Whiplash Compliment; Distinctive Oddity; and Archival, the Remix

In a Flash! **Text Reading:** The first twelve chapters of Section III, "The Liars-who-Tell-the-

Truth Club Flash Fiction," from "Spark, Spark, Light! The Inciting Incident and You" through "Archival, the Remix," pages 144-188.

Assignment: Write a flash (750 words or fewer) based on a prompt of your choice from the end of any chapter.

Week four: Spotlight on Fiction II—There's Knowing and Then There's Knowing, Cue the Doom Music, Inked, Retro-tastic Smalls, Ooh-la-la! How Intentions Deepen Character Development, The Advocate: Personality Types and Your Protagonist, The Whiplash Compliment, FOMO: Fear of Missing out & Your Characters, Tight-Roping: Balancing Self-Revelations with Self-Protection, Motley Crew: Six Questions for Your Protagonist's Pals, Beautiful Contradictions, and The Cool Side of the Pillow

In a Flash! **Text Reading:** The rest of Section III, "The Liars-who-Tell-the-Truth Club Flash Fiction", from "There's Knowing, and Then There's *Knowing*" to "The Cool Side of the Pillow," pages 189-229.

Assignment: Write a flash (750 words or fewer) based on a prompt of your choice from the end of any chapter.

Week Five: Spotlight on Editing and Submitting Flash—Tiny, Tinier, Tiniest: Tricks of Compression; Idiosyncrasies, Tangents, and Themes, Oh My!; Joy Bombs: How to Write Happy without Turning Your Reader against You; Playing Genre Ping-Pong; The Strategically-Shattered Plate; Dynamic Settings on the Skinny; The Too Timid and Tame; Plucking Posies from a Flash Bouquet: Submission Tips; Accountability Partners; Where to Submit: Market Ideas for Flash Prose; Self-Publishing and You; You Name It: Tips for Pen-Name Success; Rejection Station; Fear of Acceptance?; I Get Knocked Down, but I Get up Again; and Forever Forward: Balloon Days

***In a Flash!* Text Reading:** All of Section IV: "How to Edit and Where to Send it," pages 229-292.

Assignment: Write a flash (750 words or fewer) based on a prompt of your choice from the end of any chapter.

OR: Students may submit a revision of one of the previous four flashes you've penned during this course.

If there's a pattern to most of your assignments each week, but then you alter that pattern for a specific assignment, use different formatting (here, caps and its own line, but underlining or using red font also works well) to grab students' attention that you've changed the directions and that, in this case, students have a choice of submitting new work or revisions of an earlier piece for feedback.

Materials needed: Students will need a copy of: *In a Flash! Writing & Publishing Dynamic Flash Prose* by Melanie Faith (Vine Leaves Press 2018). This text is currently available in print and e-book copies through the publisher and online bookstores. Also, signed copies are available from the instructor—please contact the instructor if interested.

I like to list the writer (or editor, if it's an anthology) to make it easier for students to find the text and in case two books have the same title—since there's no copyright on titles.

I often list the publisher and the date of publication as well, so that students get more information about the version(s) of the text I want them to use.

Sometimes, texts are available in different editions; make sure to list which edition you prefer (since later editions often contain updated and/or omitted material from first or second editions). I sometimes also describe the color or other distinguishing feature of the cover to be as clear as possible.

I do an online search before choosing my texts to make sure the books are readily available and not out-of-print, as some out-of-print books are very expensive (sometimes over $100 a copy!), and I always want to keep my classes cost-efficient and a great value for my students. I also want to choose interesting, on-topic, and current texts since publishing (especially) has changed a lot in the past eight or ten years.

About the Instructor: Melanie Faith holds an MFA from Queens University of Charlotte, NC. Her writing has been nominated three times for the Pushcart Prize. Vine Leaves Press published her craft books about writing and editing flash fiction and nonfiction, writing poetry (both 2018), and *Photography for Writers* (2019). Her full-length, historical poetry collection set in the 1918 flu epidemic, *This Passing Fever,* was published by FutureCycle Press in October 2017. Most recently, her shorter pieces appeared in *After the Pause, Contemporary Haibun Online, The Sandy River Review, The Writer's Monthly Review Magazine,* and *Embodied Effigies.* Her flash fiction, "The Slades," placed honorable mention in the 2014 Bevel Summers Prize for the Short Short Story and was published in *Shenandoah* (Washington and Lee University). In addition to numerous photography publications, her art made the cover of both *OVS Magazine* and *Chantwood Review* in 2017. Her instructional articles about creative writing techniques have appeared in *The Writer* and *Writers' Journal,* among others. To learn more about Melanie's writing, teaching, and photography, please visit: www.melaniedfaith.com

Here's the spot for that handy-dandy bio you'll write. This is a great opportunity to list your publication credits, your website link(s), your blog link(s), recent projects, your alma mater(s), and/or your teaching philosophy. Students love to get a sense of who their instructor is as a professional writer and as a personality.

Try these exercises:

Part One: Choose one of the three or four creative-writing class topics from your Week One list to begin a sample syllabus. Using the "Sample Syllabus" chapter from this week, write your own course description listing goals/objectives based on my example.

- What will students learn overall? Consider what we've discussed about course objectives.

- What aspects of the genre or theme will you highlight during your weeks together?

- Will you use a textbook (or two)? If so, list the text(s) in your description.

- Will you write handouts? List those by title or theme, too. Even if you haven't written the handouts yet, you'll later know the exact content you need to develop your course.

- If you know the approximate length of the course, include it in your description; if not, begin to brainstorm what you think the adequate amount of time you will give the content you want to cover with fellow writers.

Part Two: Make a list of why *you* are the perfect person to teach this course. For now, some of your reasons can be silly or imaginative. The important aspect is to underscore that your abilities make you an ideal candidate to teach this subject. It's both self-motivation *and* great pre-writing that you can mine for syllabus ideas and/or phrases for your author bio. Keep your list handy and keep adding to it.

Part Three: Write a first draft of an instructor bio. Aim for 150 words or less to start. Include any teaching experiences or publication experiences relevant to your genre/class topic. Keep in mind that many great instructor bios often include both professional details and a clue or two about who you are as an individual outside of class. It's wise to avoid being *too* personal, however.

Time-Management Advice for Online Instructors

Time management is HUGE when teaching online, as mostly you'll be entirely on your own to divide up your day (or night) and balance your other part-time or full-time jobs and/or family life and/or social life.

You'll need to set aside time to:

1. **answer multiple emails or texts** (I often answer student emails and discussion boards two or three times per day, totaling up to over two hours per day, conservative estimation),

2. **offer individual and detailed feedback** on student writing (this takes an additional few hours per week),

3. **post themed and encouraging links, articles, and other writing-related content,**

4. **write course content/weekly lesson**

plans (I often write about 80% or more of my handouts and/or course lessons *before* my classes begin and then add 20% content as I go based on new themes or questions that arise in student discussion boards and/or emails from students asking about certain writing topics, once I meet my students and learn which links, books, and other resources will be most useful based on the writers' strengths, challenges, and interests),

5. **practice self-care and rejuvenation**.

As natural caretakers and encouragers, most teachers excel at the first four and make it all happen, but the caring for ourselves often gets shoved to the end of our to-do lists every day/week/month/year. It's understandable, but it's also a first-class invitation to burn-out, dissatisfaction, frustration, and inward-held anger.

Please, please, please regularly give yourself time (once a week/once a month/every few weeks) to throw aside grading, emailing, and posting in order to go have some fun.

Go to a movie, work on your own writing, eat lunch out with friends, hang out with your kids and ride bikes, hike or cycle or play basketball, go for a long drive, take a giant nap, read a giant stack of glossy magazines, listen to podcasts, whatever speaks to your heart and helps you to unwind so that you have *more* to give your student when you return in a few hours or the next day to your communicative messages, grading, and ongoing encouragement of your students' talent. I promise you: the world will not stop spinning if you pause for a few hours one afternoon.

Realize that you will sometimes fall behind on giving feedback and/or replying to student emails or posts. It happens to all of us. Be kind to yourself and honest with your students. It's best to send a quick message to students who've emailed you to let them know that you'll reply to their question shortly (I like to give a general time estimate, say "within the next three days") and then make sure you follow through. Students are super busy themselves; they are often very compassionate about the time crunch. What students *don't* tend to appreciate (and who could blame them?) is a teacher who ghosts them or doesn't give them an idea of when they might expect a reply. Don't be the Great Disappearing Teacher.

As in any classroom, there will be a great variety of students and student needs/ wants. There will be students who ask many, many questions and want more personal attention than one instructor can provide. There will also be the students who are anxious about the quality of their writing and who will apologetically email you five times if you don't immediately reply to their assignments or emails. There also be the students who go AWOL without any explanation, even when you email to check on them. Give what you can, but keep some kindness for you, too.

There is only one you; you are your writing students' greatest resource during your time together. You have something vital and encouraging to share with them—**share your personal writing stories, both the good and the cringe-worthy.**

No guilt & no judgment: it's okay, and in fact healthy, to set a few boundaries. Decide how many times a day you'll answer emails and post and how long you'll spend grading and/or offering individualized feedback. Once you've reached your personally-set daily or weekly quota, step away from the screen! I know, I know—easier said than done, and especially near mid-terms or final-project time, I've not always followed this tip as I burned the midnight oil for days on end.

Get more sleep than you think you'll need: you'll need it, especially mid-course or mid-semester.

Also: enjoy something daily that will make you laugh or smile.

Physically: stay hydrated. Eat well. Take breaks from screens to keep your body limber and your brain from dozing while wide awake.

I often break up my hour or two of morning emailing with two five-minute breaks in-between. Then, in my early afternoon I offer feedback on student work and/or grade for two hours or more, with breaks of two minutes every twenty minutes. Then I take a walk, check discussion boards, and/or finish emailing for a half-hour to forty-five minutes before hustling off to my on-campus evening tutoring job. I usually check in with my writing classes and email around 9:30 or later at night, after I finish my evening tutoring and I'm back home. This isn't a perfect schedule and it sometimes varies based on my health, workload each semester, and personal life. However, this general schedule for my online teaching keeps me in frequent, first-person contact with my students so that I have a strong online presence and can give my students care and attention without running myself into the ground.

Expect to have to give up some events for your class, especially on weekends and/or evenings. Giving quality feedback on student writing will invariably take more time than you guesstimate.

There will be people who think that because you teach online you just log in for a few minutes to play around. [Insert primal scream here.] Online teaching is as rigorous, motivating, personal, exciting, and all-in demanding as offline teaching—to both we bring vast amounts of compassion, humor, kindness, knowledge, hope, and sincerity.

It is both an honor and a calling to teach online and to teach well. You've got what it takes to share what you know and to boost both current and the next generations of writing talent.

Your words of encouragement will make a difference in the lives of your fellow writers. As writers, you will bring as much to their writing lives as they will bring to yours, however long or short your shared class.

Five Guidelines before Approaching Writers, Editors, and/or Online Programs about Your Class

Go for it—completely! Create an entire syllabus with class objectives, a course synopsis, course dates, assignments, and weekly reading. In other words: prepare the work; never just send a query letter with a vague request to teach nor just your CV/résumè alone. When you apply, demonstrate that you've put a lot of thought and care into what you'll teach and who your target student audience will be. Even if editors or recruiters end up assigning you another type of class, they'll be impressed by your level of dedication and preparation. Often, schools will be interested in running your course wholly as you crafted the sample syllabus (or with minimal changes), so make the class preparation and syllabus shine. Put thought and heart into it. **So often, the world rewards the overly prepared.**

Use it, don't lose it! Make sure you have a professional yet individualistic author bio that sets the tone for your communication style. Share this bio widely on your website, on your syllabus, and on your social media. Feel free to have two versions or more: a longer version and a shorter version especially.

Go on an updating spree! Make sure your author website and social media are current and ready for visitors. Better yet: begin your own fan page and make sure you've updated all of your social media with current content posts. If you've let it slide over the past months, no worries—but make new posts and become active again. Post the kind of resources, links, quotes, etc. that you will share with your students in the future to give possible students an idea of the quality sharing you'll do during your classes. (I post literary quotes, literary comics, literary markets links, and links to my recent publications, for instance ...) Your active online presence increases your likeability and hire-ability. Part of your job as an online instructor is to post, share, and spread the word about your classes to attract more students.

Make sure your CV/résumè is ready to go. Add your publication credits as well as all of your teaching and/or volunteering experiences. When teaching creative writing, it's often important that you have both teaching experiences and publication credits ready. Have links to your published work or sample writing prepared in case they are requested. Creative writing students want to learn from writers who actively write, edit, and pursue publication themselves. If you either have no publication credits or credits from long ago—no problem, but I'd recommend that you begin to actively send out work to editors to pursue publication so that you have that experience to discuss with your online students. Writers at all stages of the writing and publication process like to know that we're all in this writing life together, even us instructors.

Whenever possible, "chunk it." Dividing information into smaller "chunks" for students provides clear organization of the many materials involved in a class and shows students what you expect at a glance. Make sure your syllabus outlines not only a reading assignment for students but also a clearly defined, easy-to-understand writing assignment. Use plenty of dividers in your syllabus, for example, either by day, date, or week to organize weekly lessons into smaller, bite-sized objectives. When you post at an online class group or in your hand-outs, include visuals/pictures, links, and white space between ideas/paragraphs. When students scroll online, they need more white space than in print, so divide longer paragraphs (and then divide again) to be kind to students' eyes.

On Disappointment and Perseverance

My first book was not my first book. (Say what?!)

I've published five or six books (including craft books for fellow writers), three or four collections of poetry, and dozens of articles and flash-fiction stories, but the first book I wrote was not my first *published* book. Before I got a *we'd-love-to*, I got a boatload of *nopes*.

I have six finished or partially finished novels on my hard drive (including a novel set in an orchard that I wrote after grad school during National Novel Writing Month [NaNoWriMo] one November), an unpublished MFA thesis of poetry that has been rejected at least thirty times, hundreds of unpublished poems and short stories, and three nonfiction collections (including an anthology) that I'm either still shopping around or that I've permanently stored on my flash drive and retired.

Before I taught my first class online, I spent almost two years pitching classes to various online programs. That's right: let me say that again: almost two *years*. Even with a direct recommendation from a writing friend who taught for a famous online program and gave me the email of her contact, saying that I should mention she'd recommended me in my cover letter—I received crickets chirping in reply. I couldn't afford to wait around, so I kept researching online programs every few weeks and applying away.

Once I received an enthusiastic yes from Women on Writing, I knew I'd found a great fit for me, my teaching, and my writing skills. One poetry class became a personal-essay writing class became numerous classes a year.

You hear it all of the time in show business and the performing arts, but it's equally true in creative writing: there are *no* overnight successes in this discipline. Even authors who launch their own creative writing classes on their own platforms put in writing and publishing dues as well as time spent developing their courses before offering a class.

It's very, *very* common in creative writing—and in online teaching—that your first pitches and your first drafts will get polite *we enjoyed reading your work, but it isn't for us* or (more often) complete silence in response. Ready yourself for it. Ready your students for it. But how?

Here are ten encouragements that have worked to keep me moving forward when I felt discouraged or at a standstill in my writing and teaching vocations and which I often share with my writing classes to keep them motivated:

1. **Swap writing regularly with a writing buddy.** Whether it's once a week, once a month, or just when the muse strikes, having a friend on the same writing path as you can keep you producing new writing amidst the nopes.

2. **When the nopes arrive, treat yourself to a small reward for putting yourself out there and trying**—a sweet treat, a walk, an hour reading a book you've wanted to read, etc.

3. **Start a writing or teaching group.** Network tips and contacts. Swap "in the trenches" stories and goals.

4. **Jot a list of two or three more markets that would fit your writing and/or your syllabus *before* you send it the first time.** When/if the no arrives, you'll already have the motivation and know where to send it out again before talking yourself out of it.

5. **Email, text, or call a writing buddy who gets what rejection letters feel like.**

Often, writing friends understand first-hand the sting of rejection and are a great support system. They continue to submit; you will, too.

6. **Handpick motivational writing quotes online and put them up near your writing perch where you'll see them often.**

7. **Set a new goal.** For instance, if your class was just rejected for the third time, set a weekly goal to tweak the headline to make it catchier for prospective students and/or include more content to make the class sale-able before submitting it again. Oftentimes, forward momentum of any size feels good and keeps us motivated to keep pitching classes and submitting work.

8. **Tell somebody your goals.** Seriously, when I wanted to give up writing the afore-mentioned NaNoWriMo novel around the middle of the month in what I consider the "muddy middles," the fact that a few friends and coworkers knew I was taking the chal-lenge and writing the novel *and* kept asking me about it kept me from stopping. Just knowing that your non-writing or non-teaching friends might at any moment ask how it's going with your projects and class pitches will encourage you to continue. That

said, only tell people who believe in you and who will inquire supportively; there are plenty of haters out there. Your best friend, your running pal, your writing swap partner—yes, share away. Your jealous frenemy, your neighbor, the clerk at the store—probably no.

9. **Envision your teaching online as a small business.** Like all small businesses, it takes consistent effort and time to create your "product" as well as find your audience and make ongoing connections to expand your clientele. Realize that there aren't any businesses that can't benefit from more time, networking, or attention.

10. Repeat after me: you have something unique to share with online writers. **Be willing to adjust your timeline, syllabus, or approach, but never give up!**

Try these exercises:

Part One: Using previous exercises, write a class syllabus.

Part Two: Teaching online is a large investment of time and energy. Sit down with your day planner and jot notes or a list of responses considering the following:

- How much time per day/week will you schedule for posting and answering messages from your students?

- How much time per day/week will you schedule for creating new content to share with students?

- How much, if any, of your class content will you create before your class begins?

- How much time will you dedicate each week to writing and sharing lessons once your class starts?

- How much time per day/week will you schedule for offering individualized comments/feedback on your students' assignments?

- Are you more likely to have time to post content and reply to student messages early in the morning, at midday, or in the evening? Or a mixture of times?

- Be honest with yourself about how much time you really have and list ways in which you might clear timewasters out of your schedule, or at least cut back, to make more room to concentrate on your future class.

Part Two:

Craft Essays—Online Creative Writing Pedagogy Topics Megaboost

On Paper Pockets and Encouraging Writers both Seasoned and New

Remember that little paper pocket library books used to have? The one made of a slightly-thicker-than-paper oaktag of light beige? Perfect little rectangles brushed on the back with rubber paste and stuck hanging out on the inside-back cover, awaiting the blue-lined card where students scrawled their John Hancock in pencil or pen and the black stamp announced the due-back date. That index-card fit firmly into the snug pocket each time, keeping time.

Voila: a piece of borrowed magic, imaginative entertainment, was traced in the kangaroo-pouch within the very book itself—its string of readers like a necklace of pearls: the borrower who would read it until 4 a.m. the night before the big exam, the borrower who read ten pages faithfully every night, the borrower who would leave it mostly unread under a pile of clothes, the borrower who made faint little checkmarks or, very occasionally, a single word in erasable lead in the margins while sweating over a term paper.

I miss those paper pockets. Now it's all efficient barcode stickers, just as likely stuck willy-nilly on the outside back cover across the synopsis or blurbs as on the cover or spine.

Like the paper pockets, teaching blends systems of personal details and care with systems of knowledge and efficiency (borrowers knew the deal: they had to make the trek to the front desk, wait for the librarian and the black stamp, and brandish a pencil or pen to sign before departing with their treasures, not that it stopped some people from tucking tomes into their backpacks, the thrill of the illicit disappearance, especially for banned books or books on juicy topics simply too much to resist or the books one just can't bear to wait to reread— I confess, a book or two made its way onto my shelves, back in the day, this way).

Creative writing classes attract a wondrous mixture of artists with myriad life experiences.

If you have writers in class who are over thirty, they will likely recall a world whose customs, habits, entertainment, and family dynamics were much different than our world today and may want to write about these memories. Many, many students write about deceased or elderly parents. Many, many students write about beloved or rotten siblings. Many, many students write about technologies that have gone the way of the dodo in the new millennium. Many, many students write as catharsis or to exercise the demons of yesterday. Many, many students write to celebrate the people and the places they wish had not slipped from their lives. Many, many students write about people and situations that angered, frustrated, confused, or caused them to suffer mentally, emotionally, physically, spiritually, or in other ways. Many, many students write about paths to healing. This is natural, important work.

As a teacher, you will bring an outside opinion representing the literary and publishing worlds—even if you haven't published your own work yet or if you've published but not recently, you offer feedback on student work and represent constructive criticism to students and also have knowledge about why pieces of literature were publishable. As a teacher, you look for student prosody or poetry that sings off of the page and for writing that goes too general or weeps with cringe-y melodrama or nostalgia.

Yes, you'll look for grammar or structural elements, too, but most of what you offer your students will be the bigger picture, rather than smaller, nitpicky elements, such as spelling. Along the lines of: What is the main theme/point of this piece? What would make it clearer for the reader? What would I like to know/see expanded in the piece? Is this piece publishable; if not, what would make it publishable?

Often, your students don't have a literary community yet outside of you and their class, so the students' first readers will likely include family and friends who either are not skilled, professional writers, don't have literary-analysis training, or they love the writers so much that they are afraid to voice their real opinions (or, conversely, they are jealous of their writing and have given them nothing but negative or passive-aggressive feedback, which sadly happens, too). So much of what writers have heard before your class, includes tepid general feedback, such as "I loved it!" or "This is weird," or "Really great." Conversely, students' first readers might have scarred them with criticism so scathing that they are literally shaking at their nerve-ends to show their work.

Neither all-glowing nor all-dismissing feedback helps writers improve their craft.

Writers come to you as a professional who practices their craft at a high level, and offering your specific opinion can be enlightening, humbling, as well as motivating for their improvement. This is a sacred trust. Approach each student with goodwill, even if you don't personally like the student's theme, style, or tone or if they write in a genre you seldom if ever read. Your goal, for each student, is to honor how much courage it takes to show your unfinished, new work to another human; your goal is to meet your student at their present skill level and to offer real-world yet encouraging words for concrete next steps in their work.

If you have just-beginning authors in your class, whether they are newly graduated high-schoolers, college students, or writers who have longed to write for years but were stuck in jobs unrelated to their writing dreams at any age, **your goal as an instructor will be two-fold.**

Point out the elements of their drafts that are unique and/or already working well.

You know, there's usually at least one simile, metaphor, or image (even in an otherwise lack-luster piece) that shows potential. It's crucial for new writers to understand what readers find resonant in their writing, so that they can write in a way that hooks others and expands those qualities in their future writing. Also, new writers need the encouragement and support that they have some talent that can be nurtured and expanded. If you only mark everything "wrong" with a draft, not only do students tend to check out on the instructor but, even sadder, they begin to doubt their own dreams to write. Mentioning the good aspects of their writing will build their confidence in their own abilities and spark their desire to learn even more about this craft.

Don't skip the direct, clear advice. Nobody can grow with an all-glowing review.

If there's a part that confuses you or that has inconsistency with what you've read in a previous paragraph or scene, make sure to point it out—writers (myself included) often can't see the forest for the trees in our own drafts. If the writer uses mixed metaphors (as often happens in my early drafts) or if the dialogue is too wordy or shifts POV or a stanza could be divided for maximum emphasis on a particular image, mention it.

As a creative writing teacher, you will become equal parts editor, counselor, master craftsman, and (yes) authority figure—wield that power gently. We've all had teachers and professors who felt like they were gatekeepers and dream killers whose sole purpose was to let us know we'd either never be published or that we were talentless hacks wasting our time in a profession that pays almost nothing and yet where everyone thinks they can write the next Great American Novel. *But you can't. You won't with work like this,* said those naysaying educators. You will not, I repeat not, be like them. **You will offer suggestions, yes, but ultimately let the writer know that you are offering advice that is entirely *their* choice to pursue or not.** You are not offering pronouncements from on high; you are offering one educated, experience-based opinion of options that the author can choose to follow or not. The work is always the author's.

Creative writing classes, whether conferences or critiques between student authors or feedback from teacher to student, are meant to be **cooperative, two-way flows of information and suggestions.** Personally, I like to couch my suggestions with phrase like: "An idea I had that might be of interest" or "When I read this passage, I thought that maybe..." After highlighting a specific passage and making a suggestion, I might note: "Just an idea. See what you think, and go with your vision for the piece." We're not meant to be intrusive or dream-crushing in our teaching. That said, the great majority of students expect and eagerly anticipate personalized feedback. Keep in mind: it matters almost as much *how our tone comes across* when we give specific suggestions as the suggestions we are making.

I don't take it personally if students submit a second (or third) draft that incorporates few if any of the suggestions I made. It's not about my ego; it's about their drafts, and their drafts belong to them. As you grade and/or offer feedback, consider both big-picture and small-picture changes the students have made. It's important to note when writers have done an excellent job making their writing more focused and fleshed out with vivid imagery, realistic dialogue, the addition of body language, great paragraph or stanza or line progression, and the like. Also, note when students have omitted and/or compressed unnecessary details, as this is another great way to measure student growth from draft to draft.

Give the best specific advice you know how to give, based on your own learning curve with writing, editing, and/or publishing your work (students love to hear tales of their teachers' own struggles and rejections and triumphs in this writing life—feel free to include those in your comments when applicable), offer links and/ or resources that you believe will assist them, couch your suggestions with care and specificity, and then let go. Your students should not write exactly as you do; they should find their own paths with some camaraderie and some informative anecdotes from you that will assist them in choosing their own next steps in the journey.

Much as I adore and miss those little pockets (I did a photography series with an old library card and pocket from a gently used book I got online a few years ago), time rolls on and a big part of me is glad for that and happy that it's largely out of my control. As artists, as teachers, seasons have to crumple and dissolve to make room for the next and the next; it's always been this way and always will be. We practice and teach an art that is ever-mutating, ever trans-figuring with the same basic tools authors have used for centuries—word by word by word. You are a facilitator as well as a member of the writing community.

Each author will bring individual strengths, challenges, fears, and hopes to their classroom and into their work. Meet them and their writing with the dignity and goodwill you'd appreciate from readers of your own work.

Try this exercise:

Journal for fifteen minutes about the best and worst writing advice you've ever received about *your* writing. What made the best stand out as helpful? What did you glean from it that helped your writing to take off in new and exciting directions? How was the worst advice harmful, and how did you overcome it? Go!

Have You Seen These Characters?

We gingerly stuck our hands under the towels and straight into glass bowls.

"Wriggle your fingers around in it. Really give it a good wriggle!" R's mom momentarily placed her hands atop ours to encourage our hands deeper into the mystery glass bowls.

The tacky, clammy feeling of something half-cooked, long, and stringy in strands met our fingertips.

Giggles and shivers from the kid at my left.

"Ewww! That feels like *brains*!" from the kid at my right as he yanked his hand back from the cold spaghetti, although we didn't yet know that's what it was.

"It is," R's mom told us, with a dramatic flourish of a parent in her late twenties dressed as a witch, complete with green face makeup and a faux wart on her nose. "It's werewolf brains we found out behind the barn during the full moon."

"Let me feel! Let me feel!" from the third-grade classmates jostling towards the table, huddling around the next set of bowls. More jostling by more kids in pastel Velcro sneakers. "It's my turn!"

A cackle from R's mom. "On to the next station, group."

We were eager and a bit wigged out, panting and then giggling with excitement, to plunge our hands into the next set of bowls.

"Yuck!" S screamed, her pigtails set just like Pippi Longstocking's, "They're eyeballs!"

"*Real* eyeballs?!" The kids at the next table over piped in, walking to our table. "Let me feel!"

R's mom, who had peeled the skins off of a pod of green grapes an hour earlier, before we got there, emitted another quirky, cosmic cackle.

"Back to the brain bowls with you, young friends!" she shooed them away with more amusement than frustration. "We need to get through the Tarantula Web maze yet before the hayride."

Somebody started to hum the song whose last lyric we learned in music class about the coldness of having no skin.

This scene stands out to me, many years later, among numerous holiday celebrations and get-togethers of my childhood, before the complications of puberty and teen angst got in the way of living in the moment and enjoying each other's company without cliques. My classmate has two grown children and no longer lives on the farm, but every October as I get treats ready, I fondly recall my friend and that party, with those clammy noodle "brains" and the wet, round "eyeballs."

I also fondly remember the hay wagon: bundled in coats and scarves and mittens, we took three or four bumpy laps through the recently-emptied fields, the clatter of the rickety slats of the hay wagon knocking us against each other on hay bale "seats" as we laughed and some of the boys nudged extra hard for the fun of it, before returning to the toasty-warm house for chocolate cupcakes with candy corn on the top and to bob for apples in a giant metal tub.

Your students will bring their own memories to your class. That's where you step in. Writing and editing work based on events that already happened can present unique challenges to writers and opportunities for educators.

I took a day trip with a longtime friend who is also a voracious reader and a fellow educator. We discussed how even fiction frequently has sparks or observations from "real life." How could it not? The writer's art form is to observe and recreate life as it is observed—to recreate, one must first have a creation, an impetus, an observation, from which to build, even if all of the rest of a scene, chapter, stanza, or manuscript is made-up or a hodgepodge of authentic details alongside imagined ones.

Here are four common writing conundrums that you may encounter in your creative writing class and some tips for facilitating your students' stuck drafts. I've given them thematic names to keep things lively and to mesh with my Halloween motif, because ... why not?

The Vampire.

This is the writing piece that starts strong (great opening hook! Amusing dialogue! Solid conflict and tension!) and then abruptly flounders mid-to-late in the piece, as if somebody sucked the life out of all of that colorful, page-turner prose. You'll spot this problem when otherwise vivid writing goes vague and generalized when linking verbs proliferate like whack-a-moles, and when sudden omissions raise questions in the narrative (anywhere from whole characters to leaps forward or backward in a scene). In poetry, the Vampire might appear as an antici-pated ending line or stanza that doesn't create resonance, general or boring diction choices, or poems with one style or theme that then veer wildly off course. In both poetry and prose, the Vampire tends to happen when painful, unre-solved, or unfinished life events are examined. To encourage your students to go for it, I frequently highlight/note sections where the prose or verse went flat—just knowing that these are the sections where readers begin to lose interest or feel dissatisfied can be immensely helpful for writers' next drafts. Then, I often jot two or three questions that the flat writing brings to mind to give the writer some options for a possible next direction. Pinpointing vagueness and asking the writer to clarify is my one-two go-to strategy. It's often astonishing how much growth occurs between the first and second drafts with some jotted questions.

The Extra-Pretty Princess.

Everything in this draft is a neat package. Sure, the writer has a flair for word choice and creates beautiful sound patterns, such as alliteration, assonance, and consonance. And yes, there's style in their syntax or great sentence variety or pacing, but it's all glitter and twirling and fairy dust that makes a reader think: "Yeah, but what's it *about?*" There's not enough conflict to sustain a reader's interest (or there are too many conflicts and the reader's mind begins to spin or drift) if it's prose; or, there's not a clear theme or symbolism or anything beyond some imagery loosely (if at all) tied together if it's poetry. One of my favorite teachers used to call these "Beautiful Corpses" (nothing moves the reader) and another called them "Show Ponies." Whatever you call them, in my feedback to this type of writing, I encourage students to consider the larger picture since they're often very talented already at pinpointing the small details that make writing vivid. How does the writing in this new piece connect to ideas and/or themes the writer has explored or that the writer wants to explore in the future? Sometimes, I ask writers to connect an already-great image or scene in the piece to *another* image or scene. If there's not one that meshes already, they can set to work expanding their piece or adding patterns that underscore a budding theme or conflict into the piece. Along with this connective pairing (as prose and poetry both rely on artistic multiples and meaningful patterns that are purposeful and direct, rather than accidental and repetitious), I will note either that I'm not sure what the main idea of the piece is or that I believe, through context clues, that the main theme might be either _____ or _____. This advice encourages writers to think about the piece as a whole as well as to know if they are headed in a direction where the piece is salvageable. Sometimes, a draft falls apart at this stage, but that doesn't mean that the author can't begin a new draft once they've figured out what the Extra-Pretty Princess was trying to say. Writers will often "borrow" ideas from one (stalled or stunted) piece and begin a new, tighter, better one. I tell my writing clients and students that I have written about three or four key themes for the past twenty years, over and over, in different permutations and with different characters or within various genres, but that it's quite usual to work and rework ideas to refine them over long stretches of time. Rather than seeing this as a failure, I encourage my students to see this process as new growth: realizing what *doesn't* quite work and *why* makes each successive piece stronger and dramatically helps writers learn successful editing to hold their readers' attention.

The Mummy.

"All wrapped up and nowhere to go" would be the tag line for this little creature. Tell-tale signs: one character is a talking head while another character barely speaks and/or doesn't act or react. In nonfiction, this is the topic broached and then backed away from for some, if not most, of the piece. The reader gets a sense that there's more going on or much more not being disclosed, and yet there aren't enough details in the piece to flesh out the scene, background, setting, or conflict. I usually write a note that I feel like there's something more unstated going on and/or I note a passage where I felt like there was a missed opportunity for the character or narrator to explore an idea that was backed away from and what that idea appears to be or where it appears to be leading thematically but doesn't quite go in the prose. Again, the Mummy often occurs because sensitive or unresolved experiences or feelings from everyday life inspired a character or conflict in the story and so the writer isn't sure how to proceed on the page. Every creative writing teacher under the sun has probably heard (and said themselves at an earlier point in their career): "But it happened that way ... " To get around that stuck place, another gentle comment to make to authors is that they should imagine "What would happen if ... " for a ten or fifteen-minute free-write, and then add a sentence or two that they like best into the draft and keep writing from there. This exercise frees writers to approach the piece from a different angle or with details that they hadn't first thought of, much like writing a quick list. The brain can often navigate better when focusing on the forest (several options) rather than each individual tree ("this is the way it happened, so this is how it must appear on the page"). I highly recommend encouraging your students by spotlighting a specific passage or two in each assignment that they could return to for a quick free-write. Many writers have a one-and-done feeling about assignments (I felt that way myself, especially as an undergraduate writer), and just a little nudge for where and how to expand or clarify often leads to a new level of coherency and growth by leaps and bounds.

The Ghoulish Ghost who Goodbyes and Goodbyes and Goodbyes and *Never Leaves*.

This conundrum is the literary equivalent of the houseguest who overstays their welcome.

Yes, you were glad to see them and to spend time with them, but the bag's been packed and parked at the door for a long time now with nary a departure hug or *hasta la vista* in sight. Nine times out of ten, you'll spot this problem as the overwritten ending. Usually, and with good reason, the author doesn't know how it should be tied into a neat bow, so they keep writing and writing and grasping for any ideas that appear, hoping that one of them will be it. Look, beginnings and endings are tricky for almost every writer. The first thing we write is often just an entryway to get us writing and later we either move details around or edit so that our final opening is a hook that draws the reader into the piece, usually in the midst of the action (in medias res). It is often a freeing revelation that the final beginning and ending don't have to be the very first things we write in those spots—like puzzle pieces, students can, and often should, move and sculpt ideas, omitting in-between details as needed, at openings and closings. I frequently suggest to students that the natural ending for the piece is hiding in plain sight, several lines, stanzas, or pages *before* the present conclusion. I also share the camaraderie that I can spot overwritten endings so well because I frequently write them in my own first, second, and even third drafts. It really helps writers know that their instructor also has to work diligently and creatively at various parts of their craft, and it can be tremendously encouraging to talk with an author (you!) who continues to write and publish no matter what obstacles or challenges they encounter.

In the end, your goal as a creative-writing teacher should be to demonstrate to each writer that better writing is not only possible but probable if they continue to explore ideas that matter to them.

Try this exercise:

Jot down a list of three challenges you face in your own writing. When do these challenges most often occur in your own writing? How do you "fix"/work around these snafus in your later drafts?

Let's look at the obverse side; you've grown a lot as a writer, too. Let's celebrate that! Note two or three areas of your writing that have improved in the last five years. What steps did you take to reach this growth in your writing?

The next time you work with student writers, you'll have a series of these bite-sized, shareable anecdotes to encourage your students' own writing journeys.

Bridging the Gap

There can be a huge gap between what we want to write and what we actually write. We professional writers and teachers are no exceptions. There are plenty of times when I begin with a blank page that I want to fill with one idea or concept and the resulting prose is blah, boring, or heavy-handed. Back to the drawing board, often several times over, and even then ...

I have subjects or experiences I try to write about and then try again and again. For example, for three years I tutored a student I'll call HC. HC had several learning challenges, not the least of which was writing essays in a foreign language and adjusting to a completely different culture. HC and I spent many nights reviewing for history exams, writing outlines of his main ideas, memorizing new vocab, and sitting before a computer screen reorganizing his paragraphs. HC's path was not an easy one, in his personal or academic lives, and so we took it assignment by assignment and day by day.

HC's academic and personal standing rose and rose, and he made enormous strides between the first year I worked with him and his senior year. He grew a lot taller physically but also emotionally, academically, and intellectually in those thirty-six months.

During one of our sessions early in his third year, he offhandedly said that on the final night we met for tutoring, he'd play his viola for me. Months flew by and we both forgot about it—or I did. One end-of-May night, HC brought his viola case to our meeting (but sometimes, students bring hockey sticks and all matter of items to meetings, running from one campus lesson to another, so I thought nothing of it as he stashed it with his backpack under the desk). Five minutes before he was due back in the dorms, as we finished editing his last paper as a high-school student, he stopped me mid-sentence and said, "I promised you that I'd play you a song on our last meeting."

You could have knocked me over with a feather. HC might have stumbled finding the best synonym in English, but he came from a family of musical virtuosos. For four breathless minutes, his bow made magic across the strings. He played a piece of classical music whose title I don't have the slightest recall on because it took all I had to focus enough not to break down weeping at the sheer beauty of the tune that suffused the room as it danced from his bow.

It was the kindest and most meaningful thank-you gift I've ever received. HC did not have a lot of verbal articulation gifts; in fact, he sometimes inadvertently said insulting, stark, or out-of-place things when he didn't mean to, but he had brought the best of his skills and perseverance and talent to the song he had chosen to share. The second HC slammed his viola back in its case and took off down the hallway so as not to get locked out of the dorm, I wiped away the happy tears with the back of my hand.

He held himself accountable. I was touched that he'd remembered what I thought was a tossed-off offering. I was deeply moved that he appreciated what I'd offered him and wanted to give his own gift back by sharing his musical talent when he just as easily could have chosen to hold back. I've sung in a few choirs, but I sight-read and don't even remember all of the musical notes—it was an unspeakable joy to experience his facility with bringing music to life, a talent I've never possessed. It was not lost on me that he had chosen to give me his gift of eloquence.

It's already been years since that night. HC would be a college graduate and working professional by now, but for me, his gifted musical performance remains something that I've carried in my memories as if it were yesterday.

Key words: in my memories. When I've tried at least ten times to write about it, it just doesn't compare to anything I experienced even remotely, even with the paragraphs I've just written above. Yes, that is enormously frustrating. Am I always articulate on the page? Ha-ha. Off-page? Color me clumsy, and frequently. I'm thankful for the opportunity to write as many drafts as I can. Will I ever write about it as well as I experienced it? Doubtful, but who knows. Will I stop trying? You bet I won't.

I bring this up to encourage you to **share your own professional-writing stories as well as your writing**, whether excerpts or "tales from the trenches" of your own drafts, submissions, or rejection slips. We just don't know a big-enough picture of each writer's life or goals to know what advice and stories will resonate and keep encouraging them long after our classes, but we should keep sharing our own experiences whenever we have the opportunity. We never know how one supportive word or a string of funny or meaningful writing stories might make the difference between our students persevering as writers or giving up.

Students sometimes see the instructor's website or published work and think, "Yeah, well, it's easy for you." It helps student writers to mention the obstacles you personally overcame to get to where you are in your writing career. I can't tell you how many times I mention my over 700 rejection slips (no typo) I gathered while submitting poems and short stories here and there before I published a single book.

Teaching the creative arts provides unique opportunities to share our own writing struggles. **You are both mentor and fellow practitioner.** With each new piece, you have traveled the path to improve your writing and are still traveling that path. As many craft books or articles you assign (and I do love me some nonfiction craft books—I've written six so far, after all!), **you are your students' most immediate resource.**

When I first started teaching, I did everything I could so that my students would think I was an expert and to shove my flaws as far under the rug as possible. Big mistake. About ten years in (yeah, it really took me that long, egads!), I relaxed some and began to share some of my own writing, rejection slip horror stories/ badges of honor, and anecdotes about my own challenges as a student (hello, math and chemistry, my old nemesis), writer, and person. Not surprisingly now (but quite surprisingly for me at the time), students didn't question my authority now that I'd opened up. Nor did I lose face or die of embarrassment. Rather, there was a new camaraderie and respect when I shared: "Hey, I've been there; writing is an ongoing struggle for everybody, even for professional writers who love it."

You will model perseverance for your writers. You will also model the realities of the writing and publishing life, from the editing quandaries to the financial strain to the thrill of seeing your name as the byline in print.

Use prompts. Sometimes, when my students have tried several times to write about a subject that carries great meaning for them and continue to stall, I encourage them to write about something else for the next assignment. As paradoxical as it sounds, backing away from the topic can sometimes do the trick to distract our minds just enough to spark the way forward.

Whether a prompt from a craft book or prompts found online, these little one- or two-sentence set-ups can work wonders to get words flowing and reduce writing anxiety or block. I also write impromptu prompts based on a theme or idea that I know might interest a class or an individual student, based on the students' writing styles, writing goals, and their previous writing that I've read.

I frequently jot one or two thematic or character-driven questions in the margins of students' drafts and encourage students to do a fifteen- or twenty-minute free-write to see how the character would answer and/or where the draft might go next. I don't call these prompts, but yep, they are. I'm never invested in students taking the direction I'm asking about in the questions; my purpose is not to be insulted if students don't like my feedback nor to dictate what comes next in their narratives, but to bounce potential ideas and then bounce out of the picture for the writer to take the wheel again.

What I care about is that my raising potential options from what I see in the piece will encourage their own brainstorming. Plus, I understand that, as a writer, nothing is more flattering or hopeful than when a peer or fellow writer carefully considers one's work and cares enough to offer uncritical options. The way forward in a simple statement or two.

Share a before-and-after draft with your class. I've done this with several of my independent study students and with some of my classes. I choose a first or second draft and then compare it to a much-later/sometimes-post-publication version of the same piece. I often highlight or make margin notes on the first and later drafts to compare and contrast them, including such elements as omitted parts and why I omitted them, redundancies from the first draft, and plot, dialogue, and character and/or stanza or paragraph changes.

This activity subtly demonstrates for students that 1. Everybody's first drafts kinda suck (remember what Hemingway said about first drafts?) and 2. There are still plenty of literary devices for your students to apply to their own drafts before abandoning a piece forever. For example, numerous students have had "aha" moments about their own opening hooks after I showed them one of my first drafts and how I moved the fourth paragraph to open the piece instead and either omitted or moved the first opening paragraph and explained why. For many students, it can be a revelation just to know that the first sentence or image of the first draft doesn't have to (and often shouldn't) be the opening spot for later or finished drafts. This is the kind of knowledge that they can carry forward to any and all future drafts. Quite an effective exercise for all concerned!

Listen to them through it. It's my simplest tip but, in many ways, the best. As writers, there are times when we just need to gripe and vent our frustrations. Very few people in your students' lives will listen or understand the unique frustrations that accompany stalled drafts. You will. It takes extra time, but you will be surprised how many times a simple sentence or two of encouragement from you will be followed by paragraphs from your students (who will then apologize for taking your time and thank you), and then be followed by a message a few days or weeks later to update you that they are now back on track or have started writing something new. It's kind of magical how often it happens; how often just sharing their thoughts with you gets the writers back on track on their own steam.

Try this exercise:

Write a list of more shareable personal experiences you can share with your students when they are frustrated or experiencing writer's block.

Some possible topics:

How many drafts did it take to "get it right" for a piece that was eventually published?

What was your worst rejection letter?

Pick a very early draft and a later/finished draft of the same scene or stanza. Save both versions for student comparison. Jot a few margin notes to instruct students on the qualities that the later/finished draft possesses that led to its success. Extra credit for including your worst rejection letter, if you dare and still have it.

Ping-Pong or Medicine-Ball Communicators: 12 Tips for Emailing, Texting, and Answering Student Questions with Frequency

It's Saturday morning as I write. I've slept in a lovely extra hour and graded all week so that I can have today off to replenish my batteries. Glorious, free Saturday!

Well, minus the "free" part, it appears.

Opening one of my three school inboxes reveals six student messages that are rich with questions. These are multi-paragraph messages. Not one of these messages is a "yes" or "no" and done; each of these messages will take fifteen minutes or longer to answer, optimistically.

Yeah, I promised myself a whole Saturday off, but if I wait I will have two or three *hours* of emailing at the keyboard tomorrow before I begin my discussion boards and grading. I can only sit at a computer for twenty- or thirty-minute blocks before I need to stretch and move my body for my own sustained health.

I'll never get a break tomorrow if I don't give up some free time today.

I set to work this morning and promise myself that by mid-afternoon I'll be close enough to caught up that I'll get in a walk and watch a movie like I'd planned.

Sound familiar?

When I started teaching professionally in 1999, we had email but most of our communications were done in real-time and there was a more defined demarcation between teaching hours and off-duty hours. Over twenty years later, our cell phones are an appendage and the communications never stop.

One of the great crises in 21st-century education is a diminishing teacher-retention rate. How to nurture teacher self-care in an increasingly fast-paced world is a conundrum that deeply affects student writers. We've all been a student of the burned-out instructor who is snippy or who ignores students' questions altogether; it's a miserable experience for everyone involved and is not conducive to learning.

Yet, undeniably, there is pressure for online instructors to be accessible 'round the clock, which is not good for anyone's mental health.

Understandably, students should feel invited to communicate with their instructors as individualized feedback can lead to great student growth. The problem, however, is that teachers cannot be hooked to our digital devices 24/7 and still provide a warm, caring, relaxed, detailed classroom environment without health consequences, aka: burn-out.

While there's not one 100% perfect method to maintain balance, here are some great tips I've used in my own online (and offline) teaching and some ideas I've borrowed from fellow teaching professionals to cope with endless messaging.

Anticipate common student questions. If the assignment is detailed or includes many steps or potentially multiple ways of answering the same questions, get ahead of the emails by sending a group text or group email or post outlining common student questions about the assignment and give direct advice about the content you are looking for as you grade/offer feedback. I often send one, if not more, email per week to my online university classes where I outline the assignment and the various steps or parts of the assignment that several students might find confusing.

Realize that students deserve an answer in a reasonable amount of time but that "reasonable" doesn't have to mean "instant." Many schools have a policy for instructors to answer student emails within a one-day/twenty-four-hour period of receiving the mail, as one of the schools I teach at online does. Often, though, I find that emails pile up too quickly if I answer them only once a day, so I check twice a day (okay, now and again more than that). Other instructors I know prefer to answer them throughout the day or by instant notification or a text to their phones. However you go about it, decide how *you* define reasonable. Keep in mind that if you answer emails only once or twice a *week*, your students will miss out on your assistance and often may hand in the assignment late or feel so discouraged that they won't bother to do the assignment or hand it in at all. On the other hand, if being in constant contact with students leaves you depleted and jittery [let me raise my hand to that!], then work out a lower-frequency method for checking texts and/or emails.

Decide if you are naturally a ping-pong-style or a medicine-ball-style communicator. Do you savor a clear inbox? Enjoy that adrenaline rush from having made short work of answering ten messages in a row so you can go on to the next task and the task after that? Then you, my friend, are a ping-pong communicator. If this is your style, then set your phone for instant notifications and answer away all day and night as you go. If, however, you find constant notifications a distraction and would prefer a slower read-and-ruminate-before-writing method, then you are more medicine-ball-esque and should probably set aside a solid hour or two to reply, either first thing in the morning, at night, or both, instead of answering throughout the day. Personally, I don't enjoy the wired, fired-from-a-cannon feeling I get from constant texts, so I never invite students to text me; instead, I welcome emails or posts at a group discussion board. **Decide what your own personal comfort level is. Some of this might also be trial and error; adjust as you go.**

Some teachers prefer to have a video conference or a phone call, which is also a good way to communicate efficiently with students who have multiple questions so that you are not wed to your phone or laptop. Offer a fifteen- or twenty-minute conference window before you call to keep your schedule manageable and away you go!

Are the student questions long and multi-part, or are they short and sweet? Sometimes, you might have twenty minutes to reply to students and most of the questions are answerable with a link or a simple sentence or two. If that is the case, it can feel great to reply to as many messages at once if you can. On the flip side of this strategy, you will have days where most, if not all, of the messages you receive from students involve re-teaching a concept or re-explaining a theme or lesson that will need several minutes each to answer (such as before a major project, test, or other evaluation's due date). When the latter is the case, adjust your day's schedule or give up some free time in order to slow down and offer the student or students the benefit of a more fleshed-out, helpful response. You won't be able to do this every day or even with every student, so assess both your own schedule as well as when you might have some breaks, if any.

To be honest, as a natural giver, this element of answering student questions is my weakness. My natural inclination is to delve deeply into *every* student question at *all* times, but I'm running up against less energy and more tasks each day as my freelancing business continues to take off, so rather than long replies that cover every facet of a question, to-the-point replies are best. Assume the student can run with the info and research further if they need to or even ask follow-up questions. Of course, it's also a nice idea to include in the response an online article link or short video or primary source that might assist a student's learning as well.

Do a quick assessment of your texts and/ or email each day. Rank them according to importance/time-needs, and then answer a few in a row before taking a break. That student whose essay is due tomorrow (or which is past-due) needs encouragement stat while an email about a project due at the end of the week or even next week can wait until later in the day or even early tomorrow. This still gives the student plenty of time to receive your answer, research, and complete the assignment. When

I am the busiest, near midterm and final-exam weeks, I often do a quick ranking/assessment of student emails. This system works well for making sure the pressing questions are answered and gives me a breather for the less-time-sensitive queries that I still get back to, but at a more leisurely pace.

Sometimes, sleep is the answer. It's late; you have a raging headache or just can't manage one more look at a screen. Repeat after me: Tomorrow is another day. Get some rest. Wake a bit earlier tomorrow morning if you need to, but there's no reason to push yourself to an extreme. As natural doers and givers, guilt can set in but give yourself permission to power-down and rest-up when you feel completely spent. You'll begin tomorrow with more focus.

Sometimes, students just want/need some quick reassurance that they are on the right track with an assignment. These kinds of emails usually only require a few sentences, if that, and will result in continued good rapport between instructor and student. It's worth taking a few minutes to bounce ideas with a student to build student confidence; it's one of the best parts of our job as communicators. Welcome these messages. Much better for a student to reach out a few times a semester than to ignore the assignment(s) and disengage from the class.

But what about times when you are truly overwhelmed? Don't just ignore student texts or emails. Your laundry is hanging out of hampers like a dog's tongue on a hot day and you still need to grade fifteen essays before midnight and that family emergency popped up out of nowhere. No problem. Deep breath. Send a quick, kind, but direct text or email acknowledging that you have received said email and will reply shortly. Give an approximate reply time if you know it (sometimes, you won't), such as "My apologies; due to unforeseen circumstances I will be out of the office for a few hours. I appreciate your questions and will be back in touch at the earliest possible time, likely tomorrow morning or Tuesday afternoon." This message lets students know that you still care for their educational journey but that, hey, you're not a machine, people! Many students much prefer this email to receiving blank silence.

If you don't send a message and just ignore student questions, you risk either alienating students, giving off the vibe that you're too busy for them, or scaring off students from asking questions next time, none of which you intend.

Strive for positive connections with students at all times. That said, the students who will then reply five times in a row to demand your attention *right now* have been forewarned what your boundaries are and you have every right to disengage—you are a teacher, not a servant. First, do you, boo.

Set up text-free or email-free blocks in your day; you will thank yourself later. I do this trick often. I literally schedule these breaks into my day planner or on my to-do list to remind myself that they *need* to happen. Or, I make a morning list and an evening to-do list. On both of them, I "schedule" answering emails and the names of people in the order I need to answer them (based on the time limits on their queries or the order in which they emailed me). In-between those two lists—the glorious afternoon!—I can fill the time with other tasks related to teaching (hello, grading queue!) or just give myself some time to write, to read, to take a walk or exercise, to surf the 'net, whatever. Pick times in the day when you power-down your phone and live in the moment. Hey, are you listening? This bears repeating: pick a time daily to power-down and live in the moment.

Take some time off. Whether it's a weekend or a week of vacation using personal days or a semester or two off now and again, take a break if it's financially feasible. Some years, I've taken off either part or all of June or July *or* July and August to recharge my brain and batteries. I do without most luxuries to "buy back" some of my time for rest and my own creative projects; I can do without many treats comfortably, but I can't keep giving on a past-empty energy tank year after year or feel creative if I never have time for my own writing and photography.

A break, whether short or longer, renews and replenishes what I have to offer my readers and my students. Returning to my classroom for the fall semester, I'm vibrant and ready to share again. My students benefit from a more-engaged instructor. I offer more-focused feedback and enjoy the process more after a break.

Yes, take time for you. Yes, set boundaries and answer within your own time frame. Then again: go the extra mile when you can, every time you can. I know—this goes against several points I've made above. Teaching will always be an art that is underpaid, overworked, and under-appreciated by some; yet taking a few extra minutes to make another human being feel valued and on-the-right-track or to point out additional resources that might spark their writing journey will reverberate beyond the time you've spent, even if you never know about it. Students who feel cared for will sometimes write to tell you about their publication or how your class has impacted them at a time when they were at their lowest point in life—this is a part of the teaching arts that not only makes it all worthwhile but that energizes us to be meaningful communicators throughout every class we teach.

Thoughts on Late Homework, No Homework, and Life's Emergencies Big and Small

Today's the sixth or seventh day in a row of rain or intermittent snow squalls. The skies have been a blanket of gray batting for uncountable hours upon hours. I attended a funeral for a family member last week, and my high-school students just had their exam review week and took final exams. I've had two weeks of fitful sleep. The Thanksgiving feast is less than a week away and Christmas hot on its heels with all of the preparation for the season and extra events that means.

Yep, it's been *that* kind of month.

We teachers certainly aren't the only ones stressed, discombobulated, grieving, or adjusting to life's circumstances day by day and often minute by minute. Sometimes, **we and our students encounter more than we can handle and still stick to a schedule.**

Our students come to our classroom in the midst of many stages of life and often numerous personal challenges, some of which we might never know until suddenly writing assignments are missing that are usually turned in on time or the student no longer posts on a discussion board.

As a freelance teacher, you might sometimes feel a bit adrift in the storm as you message a student pulling away from the class. The following tips suggest ways to encourage their writing path and their return to class participation. The suggestions may work for students dealing with relocation, divorce, job loss, rejection slips, grief, recovering from physical illness, and the like.

When students either confide in you via email or personal message *or* noticeably turn in work that is distracted *or* turn in no writing at all, there are a few options for compassionate communication:

Offer the student a one-time extension on the assignment or project. Sometimes, it's understandable that students can't concentrate. I've offered extensions of a week or more to students recovering from the flu, experiencing insomnia or job loss, experiencing a child's hospitalization, pregnancy nausea and/ or delivery, and death in the family.

When students have reached out to me ahead of time to let me know that they are having surgery, struggling with lost childcare, moving across the state or country or world, having military deployment or job training, or a number of other events, I often send follow-up messages to check in on the student and see how things are going every few days.

Often, I send encouraging get-well or thinking-of-you memes or GIFs. The personal touch really means a lot to someone feeling alone, afraid, ill, displaced, or tired.

I also frequently offer that they may turn in just part of the assignment (whatever they've written and/or some pre-writing). Some writing is better than no writing at all, just as some prompts or assignments won't resonate with each writer each week; that's okay. Many times, after a little feedback, students report a better experience with the next week's assignment from having tried and gotten specific instructor feedback on part of the other assignment.

Look: some students will never reach out to you. It's okay to be proactive and send a quick message to say something in a kind tone, such as: "I noticed that you missed this week's assignment. I hope everything is going well, but feel free to reach out to me if you'd like a bit more time to complete the assignment." About 30% of the time, a student will reply and either explain what is going on in their life or just assure you that they will soon get the work in and apologize for the lateness. It's always the student's decision whether or not to share what is going on in their lives, but just knowing that an instructor cared enough to message them personally reestablishes a rapport and good-will between student and teacher that makes it more possible for the student to work on the assignment.

Some students will reply positively and then never turn in another assignment. Don't take it personally. It happens.

One of my best online teaching tips: I've offered students "action plans." This technique is especially helpful if students have missed multiple assignments. Often, in the midst of crisis or unrest, students don't hand in one assignment and honestly believe they will bounce back the next week, but life's demands snowball and they soon have missed two or three assignments. In this case, overwhelmed students are sometimes glad for the opportunity to see a short list of what they've missed, to have tasks broken down into smaller components, and new/adjusted due dates that they can complete in good faith over a slightly longer time period. We all get overwhelmed at times, and having someone make a suggestion and reach out with new options encourages the students that they can still finish the course on a strong note.

Yes, some students may "take advantage" and ask for several extensions in a row. I've found that these students are, by far, the exception to the rule, but it can happen. It's up to you to decide your leniency policy. For example, some writing instructors accept no late work beyond a week while others have a two-lates allowed per semester/class policy regarding extensions and after that, they will not grade or offer feedback on late work.

It's important to remember that some universities/programs have clearly-outlined policies regarding student late work and if extensions are allowed or not; check these policies online or with your academic dean, department chair, or supervisor directly.

If you're teaching for a noncredit program or offering courses on your own platform as a freelancer, you will create your own late policy. Consider what will be your cut-off point for accepting late assignments and offering feedback. Consider your own schedule as well as if/when you'll offer exceptions to your late policy. Knowing this before a semester begins will save you some stress; share your late policy with students on the first day of class in your communication, and you'll have fewer surprises later in the semester.

Keep in mind: a class or a semester is short, duration-wise. Most of my online classes and studies last just four, five, or ten weeks. The thing is, though, that making resonant art and making personal growth don't often apply to the boxes on a day planner. Just as there's no set timeframe to producing a meaningful work of art—it just takes however long it takes—there are life challenges whose reverberations are long, longer, and occasionally very long, indeed.

Some students, foreseeing weeks or months of continued chaos or confusion in their personal lives, may opt to retake the class at a more suitable time when they can concentrate and produce writing that matches their skill sets. One of the great parts of being a freelancer is that you can offer students the class at another time, perhaps as an independent study or when you run the class again, rather than a refund— and you both still win.

Caveat: if you work for an accredited school or university, there are likely already standards/ policies and regulations set up for student re-takes—consult your academic dean and/or supervisor *before* making any promises.

For classes you run on your own platform, you can work out a feasible date for your student to revisit the materials by joining a future class or to work with you directly one-on-one at an agreed-upon future time. I've occasionally offered re-takes to students in my non-credit studies who have been in the grips of child custody or divorce court, had emergency hospitalizations for themselves or their children, experienced recent parental death, or had a sudden deployment.

Hey, things pop up. Your willingness to work with student writers to reschedule or show compassionate flexibility with assignment deadlines goes a long way to building rapport and earning the loyalty of students who may either take another class with you in the future or recommend your courses to their friends. Creative writing students are vastly students of goodwill and networking.

Some writers find writing a good diversion and/or a way to process pain while experiencing turbulence and may just need a few days of hiatus to take care of personal matters, while other authors would create work they are happier with at a less stressful time. As a freelancer, you are open to discuss whatever options you feel comfortable offering.

On the other hand, in the midst of turbulence and daily changes, some students may ghost the course, even after a quick reaching-out email from the instructor. Yes, it's hard on everyone when that happens, but keep in mind that there are often embarrassing, hurtful, or life-altering circumstances unfolding in the students' lives. They might have signed up for the class long before the crisis occurred. There are times when everyone honestly needs space to process their pain and plan the next steps. Honor your students' personal journeys even when—perhaps especially when—you don't always understand the whole picture and may never fully know what occurred to pull them away from your class.

With all of this in mind, a friendly word and a kind follow-up message can encourage students during times of trial and stress more than we may realize at the time and is worth the extra effort.

Several of my students have written to me at the end of a semester, a few weeks, or even months later, to tell me that they were feeling hopeless about being so far behind on their assignments and would have dropped out of the course, but that my message(s) and an occasional extension assured them that they could finish the class.

Without sound schmaltzy, each time I received such a message touched me, and I have found myself crying tears of profound gratitude for my talented, authentic students several times. At the time, it was just an email or two to check in, but to them (and later to me) it emphasized my belief in the students and their belief in themselves—a huge outcome.

Teaching is, above all, a profession where knowledge and compassion are intertwined. The kindness you show your students with deadlines encourages connection within the classroom and may make the difference between a stalled writer and one who returns to their writing path.

In the end, we creative writing teachers are *not* here to point fingers but to connect and to facilitate the best writing possible from our fellow writers.

The Quick and Dirty Deets about Payment Methods: aka, the Shortest Chapter in this Book

One of the questions I get the most from my fellow teachers interested in teaching online is: "How will I get paid?"

Although I've experienced payment methods at the schools where I adjunct and as a freelancer, please note that I'm not a lawyer, accountant, or financial advisor, so *always* check with financial, legal, and/or banking professionals in your region to find the best options for you and your personal finances at your own discretion. That said, here are a few payment trends:

If you begin teaching for either an accredited or an independent school, I have some good news: there will be a payroll system in place. Check directly with your HR person and/or hiring representative and have them fill you in on the school's system. Many schools either send physical paper checks (although this is now fairly rare) or (more recently) a direct deposit system to your bank account, often either paying twice a month or at the beginning or end of a class. Some programs pay through an electronic transfer service.

Programs can differ widely based on if they withhold any or all of your taxes or if, instead, you are accountable for paying all of the taxes on your salary as an independent contractor (which freelancing teachers will also need to do). Your HR person and/or business office should be able to fill you in on all of these financial matters. Unless you're a whiz with money matters, consulting a personal accountant, lawyer, and/ or financial advisor about tax percentages in your area and financial budgeting tips is a wise, helpful idea.

What if you teach outside of a program as a freelancer who hosts your own classes? Writing students often prefer to pay electronically through one of several online peer-to-peer transfer services and/or mobile apps. Numerous companies offer a safe, quick, organized invoice system and charge a nominal fee per transaction. Check with your local bank and friends for the ones they recommend as safe, economical, and useful.

If I know the student and/or have worked with them before, I sometimes accept **personal checks**, which have the bonus of no immediate fee deductions for the use of the service/ transfer from companies. However, I still have to take out deductions for my quarterly taxes, as you'll have to do with all electronic or tactile payment options. Two slight caveats: checks are much slower than automatic payments and only accept personal checks from students you know personally or trust, as bounced checks carry a fine at most banks.

A quick, informal survey of fellow freelancing friends who teach and/or edit gleaned three other options:

- **Gift card or gift certificate**

- **Swap for service-in-kind** (a friend of mine has swapped tutoring and critiquing for editing services for her work-in-progress)

- **Setting up a Buy Me button on your website**. A freelance web designer could walk you through this process and/or explain more about the set-up and upkeep costs; you'd also be paying forward by supporting another freelancer

The most important thing is to have an option or two ready and set up *before* **freelance students approach you to work individually or before launching your online class.** Again, usually accredited and non-accredited schools will have a system set up already; inquire before or during the hiring process.

Also, decide if you will allow freelance students to put down a deposit and/or pay

in installments or if you want the funds upfront. I usually find it easier (and deal with less paperwork) to receive the full sum and then, after the student has paid, I pencil them into my class roster or day planner. Yet, for longer freelance projects, such as when I edit book-length projects and for a few of my independent studies, I have also accepted payment on the day class begins or partial payments—one upon registering and the rest on the day of our course.

About Planning and Preparation: Final Words of Farewell

I just bought my day planner for next year and have been entering my teaching engagements, a summer visit with my darling nieces, a week at the beach, dental and tax appointments, spring break and long fall weekend, and family birthdays. Sometimes, I transcribe with pen, other times with a clicky mechanical pencil.

It's a meaningful ritual—the picking of the planner: it can't be too big or too heavy to lug in my tutoring bag each evening or too small to fit all of my teaching appointments for each individual square, and the cover has to include a design or pattern I'll want to look at each day. The texture of the creamy ivory pages must take a variety of inks and pencil markings without too much smudging or smearing.

The filling of the weekly planner, too, is fulfilling. What events will pop up in the new year that I haven't anticipated? 2019 included some sad ones: the passing of a relative, illnesses, a friend's divorce, and also many fun ones: development of new writing courses and writing a poetry book, an auntie's surprise 80th birthday party and seeing my cousin who lives in Texas and whom I hadn't seen for seven years, a sister weekend at a bed and breakfast, a March visit to an Irish dance troupe performance with my parents, a literary reading at my welcoming undergraduate alma mater in May, walks on the beach at Topsail Island in June, publication of *Photography for Writers* in November, and a perusal through a Christmas bazaar and a Sunday afternoon play of Dickens' classic *A Christmas Carol* with a dear coworker friend who has become like a sister to me over the past twenty years. My 2020 and 2021 planners, like so many of our restricted lives in those many months, suddenly emptied of social engagements, but my squares in those planners still filled richly with my online work with talented writers through their brilliant books, short stories, flashes, personal essays, literary analysis, and poetry which helped to keep my mind well-occupied until safer in-person socializing.

Here's the thing about planners that applies so well to teaching: they don't come with a crystal ball. Not one of us can foresee what each new day, much less each New Year or semester, will bring. Teaching requires a lot of prep work, true. It is good to be as prepared as possible, with plenty of activities and prompts and reading assignments and offering as much personalized feedback and as many practical examples as possible, but in the end, the classroom experience unfolds as it will. Lean into that fact and roll with it.

Each online class and each student, like each new day, is a unique entity. There will be days when you'll sail through all of your plans, easy-breezy, and other days when you have to restate objectives and thematic examples and bring your very best lesson plans only to have to ditch the excerpts to think quickly on your feet when the classroom conversation or discussion board or a text from a student veers in an entirely different direction. **It's good to have plans for content to cover in each class but don't become locked in.**

Teaching is an often amorphous art form and is a good, if sometimes meandering, ongoing conversation. From day to day, you'll naturally assess individual writer's needs and strengths as well as the challenges when trying to offer the best and most supportive feedback that you can.

Take the time to slow down as often as possible to offer words of encouragement and instruction that might not mesh with your daily or weekly class objectives but will assist each writing student's individual path forward.

As a writer, I well remember (and I bet you, too, recall) every writing teacher who took the extra few minutes to point me in a new or exciting direction with specific constructive feedback, to underscore a passage I wrote that was clear or clever (or overly-clever, maybe) and which they enjoyed, or to recommend a writing text I might appreciate when they surely would have rather skipped off to the cafeteria, their cars and lovers and children and pets, and everything else in their regularly-scheduled personal lives.

- Be the kind of instructor who has goals but not single-minded ones.

- Be the kind of instructor who underscores what's going well with a draft as well as the areas that could use a second look or strengthening in compassionate tones.

- Be the kind of instructor who takes the extra few minutes to offer book recommendations, weblinks, and/or poetry and prose that you found inspiring in your own writing life.

Your students, too, will long remember the care you take, both with their writing and with them as individual writers. Nurture the writers and the writing improvement will often follow.

Try this exercise:

Choose one student in your class each week to send a quick, encouraging email or text that highlights an aspect of their draft or assignment that they did particularly well. This might be a message that underscores progress made since the beginning of the class, or it may focus on a writing skill one draft possessed.

Don't be too invested in the outcome. Maybe students will write back; maybe they won't. I've had some students who never reply, which is fine, too. A few students have replied that they have never had any professor who wrote just to congratulate them on a great piece of writing. Two students told me that their advisors "made" them take my class but that now they were glad that they did because they enjoyed it or learned so much. One student said she was ready to quit the class, thinking her writing was no-good, and then my message arrived and buoyed her to a solid finish. Some students have written back that they were secretly going through a personal trial and when my message arrived, it was the bright spot they needed.

You never know what a simple, direct word of encouragement will do for writers in your classes. Go forth; encourage.

Part Three:

Interviews and Helpful Additional Resources

An interview with Jessie Carty

The author of seven poetry collections. She occasionally tries her hand at prose when she isn't reading or trying to teach one of her three rescue cats to fetch. Jessie is a freelance writer, teacher, and editor in Charlotte, NC.

Q: *What inspired you to pursue online teaching?*
A: I first started teaching online at the community college where I was working full-time. I am an introvert, so teaching online gives me a chance to think about my responses in a more fulfilling way.

I've also taught online as a freelancer. This gave me the chance to connect with people not in my local community for more engaging and diverse discussions without having to worry about things like time zones.

Q: *What genres do you write?*
A: Primarily poetry but I also dabble in nonfiction with a bit of fiction writing from time to time. Same for academic writing.

Q: *Tell us about your degree and your day job. Did you have offline/on-site teaching experiences before teaching online?*

A: I have a BA in English with an Education focus and a minor in Communications. I then earned an MFA with a Poetry concentration. I also received a Post-Bachelor's Certificate in Paralegal Technology. This variety means I've had a variety of jobs, but I am always drawn back to education even when I can't find regular work. I had taught [for] about a year before I taught online. This was mostly freshman composition. My first online class was at the community college and was creative writing over the summer.

Q: *Tell us a little about how you chose the subject/theme for your course. What life and/ or writing experiences made you an expert in the field, and what was it like to share your knowledge with fellow writers?*

A: My community college courses were selected for me, but I did mostly get to design them although that isn't as much the case now. Now a lot of the online courses are pre-designed and you just facilitate them. That really depends on where you are teaching in a more formal setting.

I think being honest about imposter syndrome as a writer helped me to connect with a variety of students. And, of course, being a working writer always helps because we are all trying to connect with each other via language. I love teaching because I learn so much by working with students.

Q: *What surprised you most about online teaching?*
A: How many people will sign up for online teaching who are not tech-savvy. That can make things frustrating.

Q: *How did you prepare for your class/build your syllabus? How did you build your class content? Did you plan weekly, before the class started, or create another/hybrid system? If you could change one aspect of how you prepared or presented your class, what would it be?*
A: For community college teaching it really varied by course. For those I tend to work from what skills I want them to develop and pick assessments for that, then build the course.

For my freelance classes I planned out how many weeks I wanted to teach and then planned the topics for each week. I do prefer, in both settings, to have the whole course built before I launch it if at all possible. Then I can supplement if I want to.

I'm learning this semester as I plan a hybrid freshman composition course, that having the core of the class is great, but I want to leave myself more open to change things as needed based on the class itself. And to not be so hard on myself if things don't go as well as I'd like.

Q: *What unexpected experience(s) did you have during the class?*

A: When I taught Creative Writing 2 online one summer for the community college, I was really surprised by how different the writers were. Not even so much as what they wanted to write about but what they wanted to read. It was a good reminder that not all writers will judge what is "good" writing the same.

Q: *What did you love best about teaching your online class?*

A: The creativity of the students. I taught a Composition 2 class online that was Literature-Based and when I got to the section, I added on mixed-genre pieces. I was AMAZED by what the students came up with. From a video one posted that involved a puppet show interpretation of a prose poem to a PowerPoint graphic novel. It reminded me to try and give those creative projects when you can, even within the more traditional lessons.

Q: *What do you wish you'd known about online teaching before teaching your first class?*

A: Keep the amount of clicks low. Don't duplicate your content too often because if you have to change something you have to change it in multiple places and you will invariably miss something!

Q: *Did you learn any time management tricks while teaching your class or that you'll use when teaching your next class? How was the process of balancing life with your teaching?*

A: I made the point of checking in on my class at least once a day to keep up with everything. I find it easy to balance life with online teaching more so than face-to-face teaching which takes a lot emotionally out of me. But it is also very good to give yourself a cut-off time. Don't ALWAYS work the class just because it is online.

Q: *What's your top tip(s) for a writer seeking to break into online teaching?*

A: If you have the credentials to teach at the community college level, try picking up a class, even if it is freshman comp face-to-face, to get some experience. If you show you can do it you are more likely to be offered the chance at online classes.

Find an audience, even a small one, and try running a class very simply online so that you can put some experience on your resumé.

And network! Find those [who] are teaching online and make meaningful connections with them. Not just: TELL ME HOW TO GET YOUR JOB.

An interview with Kandace Chapple

A freelance writer and online writing teacher at Women on Writing. Her essays have been published in *Writer's Digest*, *Chicken Soup for the Soul*, *Literary Mama*, *Motherwell*, and more. She loves to mountain bike on Northern Michigan trails, hike with her dog, Cookie, and spend time with her husband and two sons. Visit her at: www.kandacechapple.com.

Q: *What inspired you to pursue online teaching?*
A: Melanie FAITH, LOL!! I had taught a few classes before on press releases but I hadn't really thought of getting into teaching personal essays—even though I do it every day for a living! After taking a couple of online classes, I realized I had something to share too. And I sought out a mentor (you!) and I decided to turn my everyday work life—editing personal essays for my magazine—into another opportunity to work with writers and earn income.

Q: *What genres do you write?*
A: Fiction, creative non-fiction, personal essays, feature stories for mags.

Q: *You just taught your first online writing class. Tell us a little about how you chose the subject/ theme for your course. What life and/or writing experiences made you an expert in the field, and what was it like to share your knowledge with fellow writers?*
A: As a writer, I know the most important thing is personal feedback. I knew I wanted to offer that in my class, that personal touch you can't get just anywhere. I have published a regional women's mag for the past fifteen years and have convinced MANY women that they TOO can write! Personal essay writing is for everyone. It's fun, it's serious, it's joyful, it's healing. It doesn't have to be published to do all those things for someone and that's what I love about it. What a wonderful thing to give yourself—your words, on paper, somewhere, forever!

Q: *What surprised you most about online teaching?*
A: I had a very experienced writer sign up for my class, and I felt intimidated! I thought I would get only beginners. But she had already published books. I thought the content would be too basic for her—but it turned out that she

was the best student—not because she was an awesome writer (she was) but because she WANTED to learn more! She had the heart! The personal feedback is valuable at any stage of your writing life. Also, she reminded me that you never stop growing as a writer. Every piece can be a challenge and a chore or a triumph too!

Q: *How did you prepare for your class/build your syllabus? How did you build your class content? Did you plan weekly, before the class started, or create another/hybrid system? If you could change one aspect of how you prepared or presented your class, what would it be?*

A: I should have prepared my classes entirely ahead of time. Instead, I worked about a week ahead of the group. The plus to this is that I found myself tweaking my content to fit their needs. But I wish I had the bulk of it written, with the idea that I added/tweaked as needed. I tried Googling other online classes like mine but saw that everything online was just an echo of everything I'd ever heard about writing! SO, I turned inward and thought: *What have I learned*?!! It turned out that the bulk of my content was based on personal experience, anecdotes, how I got published, where, what it's like to work with an editor, that kind of thing. I also offered advice based on the kinds of questions I've rec'd as an editor over the years.

Q: *What unexpected experience(s) did you have during the class?*

A: I was surprised at how quiet my FB group was! It was only seven students, but I expected them ALL to reply! Only about three were active online (but six sent in assignments). It was kind of lonely. LOL. I wonder if it would have been smarter to do just emailed lessons so that the other student's apathy didn't affect the group? I might have gotten more interaction with the personal nature of email. But on the other hand, I didn't want my inbox flooded with chatter. I had to keep a professional distance so to speak!

Q: *Has online teaching a creative art enhanced your own writing? If so, how?*

A: I was intrigued at all the different writing I did get. It made me realize that every voice is different. I was like wow, I have a VOICE! Does that even make sense? But it was like this little epiphany to see all these women be so different but working from the exact same lesson. It inspired me—that my voice is mine alone, and I have something to offer, as do they! The beauty of everyone's VOICE really hit home with me!

Q: *What did you love best about teaching your online class?*

A: I loved the convenience of working whenever on it. I loved being in charge, haha!

Q: *What do you wish you'd known about online teaching before teaching your first class?*
A: I had been warned that one to two students would "disappear" and that turned out to be true! SO, I was glad I was forewarned (by you!).

Q: *Did you learn any time management tricks while teaching your first class or that you'll use when teaching your next class? How was the process of balancing family life and your day job with your teaching?*
A: I did find that it took more time than expected to reply individually to students. I needed to allow more time for this class. I had seven students, made $700. In the end, I don't know if that was a lot of money for the time it took. My per-hour rate will increase though if I reteach this class. I would say there has to be a "long game" to it to make it worth having to create so much content from scratch. So, advice would be to create classes you can use again or in another arena.

Q: *What was your application process like? Did you apply to more than one school? How did you find out about Women on Writing? How much time elapsed between coming up with your class, pitching it, and teaching it after acceptance?*
A: I applied to Women on Writing, and it just happened to be right before their deadline for fall class proposals. I heard a reply in about a week

and they said yes. I was shocked, LOL! They told me I could pitch spring classes but not until they surveyed my first round of students. I got positive feedback (yes!!) and pitched two classes to WOW, and they accepted both for spring. I did go on to pitch the online class to two arts centers in my town—as in-real-life classes—I am waiting to hear back on those. These classes ask for 30% of the classes' fees. So that's similar to WOW and felt fair.

It did not take me long to write up the class proposal—maybe two to three hours? It was a basic outline, and I mimicked the format they already used online, tweaking it to make it my own. Bio, enticing first paragraph, brief outline of each week at a glance. My advice is to visit their website and mimic their style with your own personality, interests, and individual information. Make it as easy as possible for them to say "yes" and already "see" your class on their website.

Q: *Will you continue to teach online? If so, what class(es) will you offer next?*
A: I will re-run my personal essay class – like I said before, the bulk of the work is done! I also added a "part 2" class for my personal essay writers to take the following month if they want to keep writing/have accountability now that they are started on the personal essay gig!

Q: *What's your top tip(s) for a writer seeking to break into online teaching?*

A: Study their website. Do you fit? Would you TAKE their classes? Do you respect what they are doing and how they have it set up? I would be sure to align yourself with an organization that does a nice job!

Take a class or two. Get experience being the student. What works, what doesn't? Mimic a format you like and make it yours depending on what you liked/didn't.

Be sure to pitch a class you want to spend hours on. Your students will catch your enthusiasm! Even if they struggle with content, I think encouragement is really what they are seeking! It's fun to get people excited about their interests!

An interview with Kristine Tucker

A veteran teacher with nineteen-plus years of classroom experience. Her interest in humane education, expressive arts, adult learning, literacy, special education, sustainability, outdoor/experiential education, and transformative learning is indicative of her deep commitment to social change. Kristine has worked as an elementary education teacher, middle school teacher, special education teacher, literacy coach/staff developer, and college professor. She is co-author of *The Literacy Leadership Handbook: Best Practices for Developing Professional Literacy Communities* and authored her doctoral dissertation, *Teaching Through the Lens of Humane Education in U.S. Schools*. Kristine works as a full-time educator at Ridge and Valley Charter School and as a faculty mentor with the Institute for Humane Education at Antioch University www.creativewritingwithkris.com.

Q: *What inspired you to pursue online teaching?*
A: My initial source of inspiration grew out of my own love of online learning. I decided to work on a doctorate in higher education at Walden University and an adult learning and a graduate certificate in humane education, both program pathways were online. I quickly discovered the benefits of online learning for myself and wanted to participate in this movement as an online educator. Soon after completing my graduate certificate in humane education with the Institute for Humane Education (IHE), I was invited to be a faculty mentor for students in the program. Quickly, I learned the benefits of being an online instructor. My love of learning and teaching/mentoring online evolved almost simultaneously.

Q: *What genres do you write? Do you practice other arts as well?*
A: I love to write nonfiction, flash nonfiction, flash fiction, and recently, I've become quite enamored with micro-memoir writing. In addition to writing, I love to paint, especially within the niche of intuitive abstracts.

Q: *Tell us about your degree and your day job. Did you have offline/on-site teaching experiences before teaching online?*
A: I've been an educator for nineteen-plus years and currently work at a K-8 school with a mission

and vision supporting sustainability and outdoor, experiential learning. In addition, I'm certified to teach elementary education and special education. I've also served as a reading coach and staff developer.

Q: *You just taught your first online writing class. Tell us a little about how you chose the subject/theme for your course. What life and/or writing experiences made you an expert in the field, and what was it like to share your knowledge with fellow writers?*

A: In my affiliated IHE role as faculty mentor, I designed a writing course, Writing for Personal and Social Change, which I continue to facilitate online. I chose this subject and theme as it was a natural extension of the themes explored across the course courses in the humane education program. With a focus on environmental ethics, animal protection, human rights, and culture and change, Writing for Personal and Social Change offers an opportunity to explore writing as an expressive arts form and pathway for inspired action. Having written a doctoral dissertation focused on humane education and having co-authored a book on literacy leadership, these were two important experiences wherein I acquired a felt sense of what it means to move through the creative process as a writer, educator-activist, and cultural creative. What I love most is supporting others in their journey, serving as facilitator and guide.

Q: *What surprised you most about online teaching?*

A: What surprised me most about online teaching is the community experience, depth of learning, and relationship-building that is absolutely possible in this niche.

Q: *How did you prepare for your class/build your syllabus? How did you build your class content? Did you plan weekly, before the class started, or create another/hybrid system? If you could change one aspect of how you prepared or presented your class, what would it be?*

A: When I designed Writing for Personal and Social Change, I first created a description of the course which thereafter served as an anchor experience and guide to select books and films integral to the vision and desired learning experience outcomes. Then, the rest of the syllabus was created in alignment with program and university guidelines. This process, and all I learned throughout the course with Melanie, Creating an Online Creative Writing Class for Fun and Profit, provided me with the knowledge, skill, and confidence to design and launch my own website platform with several course experiences available for adults who want to explore what it means to write and to live a writing life.

Q: *What unexpected experience(s) did you have during the class?*

A: I am always open to shifting and changing

what's happening in a course based on participants' interests and needs and because of this worldview and approach, not much is unexpected. I embrace the unexpected and expect it, welcome it, invite it, so what emerges never feels like an upset or a negative. I find that this approach deepens the experience for everyone involved.

Q: *Has online teaching a creative art enhanced your own writing? If so, how?*
A: Yes, absolutely. My life is enriched because of the interactions, community, and learning that occurs within the courses. Therefore, my own writing and expression is enriched as well.

Q: *What did you love best about teaching your online class?*
A: I love being an entrepreneur. I love all facets of creating content, sharing that content, supporting writers, and nurturing community connections via social media. I am meant to be living and helping in exactly this way. This lifestyle resonates deeply.

Q: *What do you wish you'd known about online teaching before teaching your first class?*
A: Above all else, I do believe that for me, the process unfolded exactly as it was meant to unfold. I have no regrets, nor any wishes to have known something sooner than I learned it. This is the journey.

Q: *Did you learn any time management tricks while teaching your first class or that you'll use when teaching your next class? How was the process of balancing family life and your day job with your teaching?*

A: A supportive network of family and friends is integral when working full time and also teaching online. In addition, my love for this work and positive outlook continually provides momentum and inspiration is all around. Project management is key and integral to the creative process. Most of the time, I work from my own wellspring of health, wellness, and intuition.

Q: *Will you continue to teach online? If so, what class(es) will you offer next?*

A: I do plan to continue teaching online and plan to design new courses. I'm not sure what will be next and that is very exciting!

Q: *What's your top tip(s) for a writer seeking to break into online teaching?*

A: It has been so helpful, so very important to have Melanie as a mentor. Therefore, my top tip is exactly that—connect with a mentor who has already accomplished what it is you seek to accomplish and learn as much as possible, while also giving back.

Commonly Asked Questions about Launching as a Freelance Teacher

Q: *Do I need a website to begin teaching online?*
A: No, it's certainly not required, and in most cases it's entirely up to you. (Although, if you're applying to teach at an online accredited or non-accredited school, always check their application guidelines to make sure of requirements.) Some writing teachers keep a blog (another option), while others maintain some social media.

On the other hand, it's a very smart idea to have an author website in place as a freelance business person. I began teaching online without a website and didn't have one until about three years ago. On the other hand, I started teaching online on the ground floor when getting an author website was still a relatively new idea. In the past five years, especially, almost every writer in every genre I know has established a web presence, which includes a website 85% of the time.

Students can get a feeling for your personality, communication style, and your prose or poetic voice through your website. While the schools I teach for online don't require an author website, many of my students later report looking me up via my website or social media (or both) before signing up for my classes or writing studies or perusing my website during our first weeks of class. After seeing the links to my books, several of my students have graciously bought copies of my books, even when they weren't assigned as part of our class syllabus. A website is a great way to collate clips of your published writing, your bio, your blog (if you have or want to start one), and your publication news all in one place for employers and editors as well.

The content you share on your website can offer students a great insight into your class-room and teaching style and attract writers who might have been on the fence about taking your course. Why not put your best foot forward and show 'em what you've got?!

A website is surely an investment of precious time and money, but (at least for me) it continues to reach out to students and editors in ways that I couldn't with just an email. I have often used my website link as part of my bio when submitting manuscripts to publishers as well.

Q: *Should I narrow my online class to a certain age group or demographic that matches my writing or my professional teaching experiences offline?*

A: Certainly, it can be wise business-wise to find a target audience that meshes well with the publications you've already had and any classroom experiences you already have. For instance, if you write children's picture books and teach nursery school, then marketing your online course to parents and the pre-school and K-5 set makes great sense and will likely yield new social media followers, readers, and perhaps even increased sales and reading engagements for your books.

That said, you can target your class to any genre or market you wish as long as you are passionate about the material and have insights to share. I taught high-school students for nine years before pitching my first online poetry class to adult writers, many of them college graduates. I did not let it stand in my way that my primary teaching experiences at that point were with teenage writers instead of working professionals. I had published two chapbooks of poetry and poems in numerous magazines, had continued to write in the genre, and had studied for an MFA, so I had plenty of insights to share and passion for my subject matter. A few years later, I interviewed and was hired to teach graduate students online.

Q: *Is teaching online a flexible part-time gig?*
A: Yes, absolutely. I love the freedom of making my own schedule and of never knowing, from week to week, exactly what tasks each day will contain—online teaching provides marvelous variety in content and interpersonal interactions.

Plus, if I want to go to the store at 10 a.m. before it's busy but grade for my online students at 9:30 at night, I can. With online teaching, I also don't have to coach sports or be an academic advisor or lead clubs—I get to focus on the main event of creative writing, which feels great.

Many of my online teaching friends are mothers or fathers who like that they can pick their kids up from school, attend recitals and practices, and get work done late at night or early in the morning. Sometimes, online classes are asynchronous and involve message boards or private groups where students and faculty can post and reply at their convenience. Podcasts, links, and recorded videos have also enhanced the time-saving, connective teaching tools for the online classroom.

That said, to paraphrase Gertrude Stein, "teaching is teaching is teaching." Whether online or offline we teachers often invest almost full-time care and energy into courses behind the scenes in preparing course materials, offering personalized feedback, answering students' questions and emails or texts, and other teaching tasks. Just because online teachers have scheduling freedom doesn't mean we also don't have overflowing obligations and schedules that are packed.

Like any part-time job, to have an engaging and motivating creative-writing classroom online, just as in any brick-and-mortar classroom setting, you'll get as much out of it as you invest into it. We teachers often invest a great deal more of ourselves and our time for the benefit of our subject and, more importantly, our students' growth.

Going in, realize that there aren't any shortcuts to teaching online and that some weeks you'll spend more time than you anticipated at the keyboard or tablet, depending on courseload, student questions, quality of student drafts, and a number of other factors that can be hard to anticipate.

Additional Reading and Resources to Explore

Articles and PDF booklets:

"Creative writing in the classroom: five top tips for teachers" by Alan Gillespie: https://www.theguardian.com/teacher-network/teacher-blog/2013/sep/26/five-tips-creative-writing

"Guide to Teaching Online Courses" by the National Education Association: http://www.nea.org/assets/docs/onlineteachguide.pdf

"How to Be a Better Online Teacher: Advice Guide" by Flower Darby: https://www.chronicle.com/interactives/advice-online-teaching

"So You Want to Teach an Online Writing Course?" by Jane Friedman: https://www.janefriedman.com/want-teach-online-writing-course/

Books:

There are innumerable creative writing texts for inspiration and prompts in many genres. An online search with keywords within the genre you teach will yield a bevy of other excellent options as well. **This list, therefore, will focus on pedagogy-related books (alphabetized by title):**

101 Creative Writing Exercises (Adventures in Writing) by Melissa Donovan

A Professor's Guide to Writing Essays: The No-Nonsense Plan for Better Writing by Dr. Jacob Neumann

Creative Writing 101: Lessons from an Innovative Classroom by Stuart Albright

Don't Forget to Write for the Secondary Grades and *Don't Forget to Write for the Elementary Grades,* by 826 National, Jennifer Traig, et. al.

How Dare We! Write: A Multicultural Creative Writing Discourse by Sherry Quan Lee

Teaching Creative Writing: Ideas, exercises, resources and lesson plans for teachers of creative-writing classes by Helen Stockton

The Practice of Creative Writing: A Guide for Students by Heather Sellers

The Writing Teacher's Companion: Embracing Choice, Voice, Purpose & Play by Ralph Fletcher

Write Like This: Teaching Real-World Writing Through Modeling and Mentor Texts by Kelly Gallagher

Writing with Mentors: How to Reach Every Writer in the Room Using Current, Engaging Mentor Texts by Allison Marchetti and Rebekah O'Dell

Professional teaching organizations:

National Council of Teachers of English (NCTE)

National Education Association (NEA)

Websites for Genre Resources:

The Poetry Foundation

Poets & Writers Magazine Classifieds

Writer's Digest

Acknowledgments

To my dream team at Vine Leaves Press, many thanks! Jessica Bell for the fantastic encouragement and sublime cover designs, and Alexis Paige for developmental edits that were both insightful and fun and for the rad Gen-X camaraderie (a hearty Bravocado to you! #teambravocado). Always a pleasure to work with you. Many thanks also to Amie McCracken and Vine Leaves Press copyeditors and proofreaders for the additional polish that crossed any Ts and dotted any Is that I'd missed.

This book was inspired by a class I developed and taught for Women on Writing. My thanks to my talented, inspiring editors, Angela Mackintosh and Marcia Peterson, who are always enthusiastic and supportive of the various classes I've dreamed up, developed, and taught over the years.

Special thanks to fellow educators Jessie Carty, Kandace "Kandy" Chapple, and Kristine Tucker for your meaningful and helpful responses about your online teaching experiences. Much appreciation to Gina Troisi, Fred Leebron, and Terri McCord for reading this book when it was still a manuscript and for writing wonderful blurbs in support of it.

As always, many thanks to my parents, Thomas and Linda Faith, and my sister, Amanda McGrath, and her family—Adam, Cora Vi, and Sylvie Ro, for being my cheering section through this ongoing writing and teaching life.

This book is for my fellow teachers, writers, and students who continue to inspire and motivate my own writing and teaching.

This book is also for *you*, dear reader, and the classes you'll teach online. Go get 'em!

Vine Leaves Press

Enjoyed this book?
Go to *vineleavespress.com* to find more.

CPSIA information can be obtained
at www.ICGtesting.com
Printed in the USA
LVHW030953220122
709067LV00004B/216

9 781925 965780